A Brief History of Protestantism in the United States

Robert C. Jones

Robert C. Jones
POB 1775
Kennesaw, GA 30156

robertcjones@mindspring.com

First Edition

ISBN: 1450510671
EAN-13: 9781450510677

This book is dedicated to the Christian History and Theology Sunday School Class at Mars Hill Presbyterian Church, Acworth, Georgia

Thanks to Susan Baker and Debra Kasson-Jones for their proofreading assistance on early manuscripts of this book.

Contents

CONTENTS..4

INTRODUCTION...5

PART ONE INTRODUCTION 8

CHAPTER ONE – 1500S & 1600S............................11

CHAPTER TWO – 1700S...14

CHAPTER THREE – 1800S..24

CHAPTER FOUR – 1900S..36

CHAPTER FIVE – 2000S..56

PART TWO INTRODUCTION....................................59

CHAPTER SIX - ANABAPTISTS.................................60

CHAPTER SEVEN - ANGLICAN CHURCH.................64

CHAPTER EIGHT - BAPTISTS...................................69

CHAPTER NINE - LUTHERANS.................................72

CHAPTER TEN - METHODISTS.................................79

CHAPTER ELEVEN - PENTECOSTAL MOVEMENT.........85

CHAPTER TWELVE - PRESBYTERIAN CHURCH.................88

CHAPTER THIRTEEN - UNITED CHURCH OF CHRIST.........97

SOURCES..100

Introduction

This book is a handbook on the history of Protestantism in the United States. Part One of this book will look at broad Protestant movements, including revivals, social movements, and the evangelical versus social gospel debate that has raged at least from the time of the Civil War until today. Part Two focuses on Protestant history through the prism of the Protestant denominations, including their (mostly) European roots. Note that in both parts, I from time-to-time include Roman Catholic events in the time lines as a comparison.

A starting point for examining the history of Protestantism in the United States is to look at what binds most Protestants, and what separates them. A brief summary of these issues can be found below.

Areas of agreement among Protestants

Most Protestants today in the United States accept the basic Creeds of Christianity, including the Apostles and Nicene. Most agree with Luther that we're saved by faith alone through Grace − not through anything we do ourselves. Most Protestants believe that no intercessor is needed between an individual and God ("a priesthood of believers"). Almost all Protestants believe that only the Bible is the divinely-inspired Word of God − not the writings of, for example, the Early Church Fathers, as significant as they are.

Areas of disagreement among Protestants

Even with this strong basis for agreement, there were still many areas of disagreement that caused the proliferation of denominations that are still with us today. Among those areas of disagreement:

Practice	Choosing sides
Believer's baptism vs. infant baptism	Baptist, Anabaptist vs. Presbyterian, Methodist, Anglican, Lutheran, UCC
Immersion vs. sprinkling	Baptist, Anabaptist, some Pentecostals vs. Presbyterian, Methodist, Anglican, Lutheran, UCC
Relationship between church and state	Anabaptists believed in strict separation
The meaning of the Eucharist (Communion)	Transubstantiation - Roman Catholic Church Consubstantiation - Martin Luther Symbolic - Ulrich Zwingli

Practice	Choosing sides
	Spiritual - Caspar Schwenckfeld
Free will vs. predestination	Methodist vs. Presbyterian
Eschatological beliefs	Baptists, Pentecostals tend to be premillenialists
Pacifism	Anabaptists believed in strict pacifism, as did early Pentecostals
Role of the Holy Spirit	Baptists, Pentecostals, Methodists vs. Presbyterians ("Frozen Chosen"), Anglicans, Lutherans

In addition to doctrinal differences as outlined above, Protestants in the U.S. have also been divided on other issues such as:

- Style of worship (charismatic versus liturgical)
- "Spirit-filled" versus rationalist
- Should the Bible generally be taken literally? Is the Bible inerrant?
- What is the most important message of the New Testament (Social Gospel versus salvation-focused)?
- Is Jesus the Divine Son of God, or just a "good man" or a prophet?

Part One – Revivals and Movements

Part One Introduction

Part One of this book will look at broad Protestant movements, including revivals and social movements. Often these movements and revivals were not connected to any one denomination, or group of denominations. Part One will also discuss the evangelical versus social gospel debate that has raged at least from the time of the Civil War until today.

The Evangelical/Social Gospel debate has spawned a lexicon all of its own. Some of the more common terms are defined below.

Charismatic – Generally refers to a style of worship that is "Spirit-filled" and non-liturgical. It often involves the use of modern music and electric instruments, but not always. Charismatic worship has been around at least since the 19th century revivals, but it really took off with the rise of the Pentecostal movement in the late-19th and early-20th centuries

Fundamentalists – Generally believe that the Bible is meant to be taken literally, and that the Bible is inerrant (i.e. there are no mistakes in the Bible). The American Fundamentalist movement came into the public eye during the Scopes Monkey Trial in the 1920s.

Mainline denominations or **mainline churches** – This one is a little harder to pin down, but the use of the term "mainline denominations" is typically referring to Protestant denominations that started in the Northeastern part of the United States, and have grown increasingly "liberal" over the years. These might include Presbyterian Church U.S.A., United Methodist Church (which at one time was a young upstart denomination in both the United States and England), Anglican/Episcopal, Lutheran and United Church of Christ. Northern Baptist churches are sometimes included in this category. Mainline denominations or churches are typically in the "Social Gospel" school of thought, believing that the key message of the New Testament is "love thy neighbor".

"Social Gospel" – Social Gospel Christians (often associated with mainline denominations/churches) believe that the key message of the New Testament is "love thy neighbor" and the Beatitudes. They often view that the primary role of the New Testament is to provide a roadmap for righteous living. The saving grace of God, Jesus as the Divine Son of God, and eschatological themes are typically not emphasized. Social Gospel advocates are often more focused on what Jesus said than on who he was.

Evangelical – This is the hardest one to define, because it means so many things to so many different people. The mainstream press tends to use this synonymously with "Fundamentalist", but many Evangelicals are not Fundamentalists (most Fundamentalists are Evangelicals, though).

So, what does it mean to be an Evangelical? The term was used by Martin Luther to describe the key precepts of Protestantism, which include:

- All mankind are unregenerate sinners - there is nothing that man can do on his own to achieve salvation
- Sin is a massive gulf between God and humans - God sent his Son, Jesus, to redeem the sins of mankind
- Through faith in Jesus, humans can become reconciled (justified) with God
- Salvation for humans beings is through the grace (unmerited favor) of God only - No one is worthy of salvation
- Mankind is not saved through works - works are a result of justification, not a cause

So, if you believe those things, you can refer to yourself as an Evangelical.

However, the term "Evangelical" in modern times (at least in the United States) carries other connotations than simply believing in the key precepts of Protestantism promulgated by Luther and Calvin. These could include:

- Evangelicals typically put a strong emphasis on the saving grace of God, Jesus as the Divine Son of God, and eschatological themes
- In many Southern denominations and churches, "Evangelical" is synonymous with "being born again", or having a conversion experience. However, it is possible to be an Evangelical without putting emphasis on a "born again" experience (many Evangelicals were raised Christian from birth, were baptized as infants, and have never had a "conversion experience").
- To many people, "Evangelical" is synonymous with the ministry of Billy Graham, although he certainly didn't invent the concept. American Evangelical predecessors of Billy Graham include Jonathan Edwards, George Whitefield, Dwight Moody, Francis Asbury, John Darby, and Billy Sunday.
- In the last 25 years, "Evangelical" has also taken on a political connation, as the elections of Ronald Reagan and George W. Bush to

the presidency is often attributed to "Evangelicals". However, not all Evangelicals are Republican.

"**Conservative**" versus "**Liberal**" (or "Modernist") – when these terms are used in the context of modern Protestantism, conservative is often synonymous with Evangelicalism (and its emphasis on the saving grace of God the Father, Jesus as the Divine Son of God, and eschatology), while "liberal" is often synonymous with "mainline" churches/denominations that preach a Social Gospel. In this context, these terms are not synonymous with political affiliations. For example, many black churches are conservative from a theological viewpoint, but liberal from a political viewpoint.

To sum up, Part One of this book will necessarily need to address the tensions described above – Spirit-filled versus rationalist, Evangelical and/or Fundamentalist versus Social Gospel, and charismatic versus liturgical.

Chapter One – 1500s & 1600s

1500s

Date	Event
1565	First permanent Roman Catholic parish established in America at St. Augustine, Florida
Late-16th Century	Franciscan priests found a series of Roman Catholic missions in Florida, and along the Gulf coast
1598 - 1680	40 Roman Catholic missions established in New Mexico

In the new world, Christianity was represented in the 1500s primarily by the Roman Catholic Church, with late-16th century churches established in Florida, the Gulf Coast and New Mexico, as Spain increased its presence in those areas.

Protestantism, for all intents and purposes, didn't exist in the Americas during the 1500s.

1600s

Date	Event
1607	First congregation at Jamestown (Anglican)
1611	First Presbyterian congregation in America, in Virginia
1619	Lutheran service at Hudson Bay
September 6, 1620	Pilgrims embark for America aboard the Mayflower (Congregationalist)
1630	Puritans embark for the New World (Congregationalist)
1636	Massachusetts Bay Colony votes to give £400 to establish a college in Cambridge, MA, named after early benefactor John Harvard (Congregationalist)
1639	Separatist minister Roger Williams establishes a Baptist church in Providence, Rhode Island (Baptist)
1662	Massachusetts adopts the "Half-Way Covenant", relaxing rules limiting church membership (Congregationalist)
1677 - 1683	William Penn, an English Quaker, establishes Pennsylvania ("Penn's Woods") as a haven of religious tolerance
1683	Mennonites settle in Germantown, Pennsylvania

Date	Event
	(Mennonite/Amish)
1689	Puritan charter is revoked, guaranteeing other religious groups (Quakers, Baptists, Anglicans) religious freedom (Congregationalist)
1691 - 1692	Witchcraft trials in Salem; 19 executed for witchcraft (Congregationalist)

Protestantism began to flourish in America in the 1600s as denominations including Anglican, Presbyterian, Lutheran, Baptist, Congregationalist, Amish/Mennonite and Quakers established a presence in the new world, mostly in the northeast and Virginia. Religious tolerance was an issue throughout the century, as the Congregationalists in New England established restrictions on other denominations. William Penn would begin his grand experiment in religious tolerance in Pennsylvania, and would attract many Protestant groups including the Amish/Mennonites, Lutherans, Presbyterians, Schwenkfelders, German Reformed Churches, and the Seventh Day Baptists.

The Landing of William Penn[1]

William Penn (1644 – 1718) was an English Quaker who longed for freedom to practice his religion without persecution (he was jailed once in England for publishing a tract questioning the doctrine of the Trinity). William Penn would receive his wish when, after the death of his father (Admiral Sir William Penn), King Charles II of England granted the young Penn a vast tract of

[1] Library of Congress LC-USZC4-12141

land west of New Jersey in America. Penn would go on to create a haven for religious dissidents (especially German religious dissidents). Penn personally designed the greatest city of Pennsylvania ("Penn's Woods"), Philadelphia ("City of Brotherly Love"). Penn lived in Pennsylvania for several years, and built an estate in Bucks County called Pennsbury Manor.

The Congregationalists have as their ancestors the Puritans. The Puritans were a group within the Anglican Church that wanted to "purify" the church. More radical elements of the movement were called Separatists, who advocated a clean break from the Church of England.

In 1620, the Pilgrims, a radical offshoot of the Puritans, set sail for America on the *Mayflower*. Following close behind them in 1630 were another group of Puritans which established a colony in Massachusetts. These two groups would have great influence on religion and government in New England for the next 100 years.

Congregationalists believed in local autonomy for churches, adopted a Presbyterian form of government on a regional and national level, and were strict Calvinists. In fact, in the early years, Presbyterians and Congregationalists were closely associated in the Northeastern part of the United States.

The strong Calvinist roots of the early years of America/United States were sown in the 1600s.

Chapter Two – 1700s

Date	Events
18th century	• Split among Baptists into "Old Lights" (rationalists) and "New Lights" (more focused on the impact of the Holy Spirit and emotionalism) • Black Baptist churches begin to be formed in the South
1706	First American Presbytery at Philadelphia (Presbyterian)
1734	Jonathan Edwards is a key figure in the Great Awakening in the United States
1735/37	John & Charles Wesley minister in Georgia (Methodist)
1740	Presbyterian Church splits over feud between "new side" revivalists and "old side" Calvinists (Presbyterian)
1740	Methodist George Whitefield arrives in America, and spreads the work of the Great Awakening through America
1757	Presbyterian reunification from the 1740 split
1766	First Methodist Societies in the U.S.
1769-1771	John Wesley sends lay ministers to the Colonies, including Francis Asbury (Methodist)
1769	Junípero Serra founds Mission San Diego de Alcalá at San Diego. Eventually, a total of 21 missions would be established in California, the last in 1823. (Roman Catholic Church)
1770	Mother Ann Lee (1736-1784) has a revelation that sex is at the root of all human evil; celibacy becomes foundation of Shakers
1775 - 1783	Disarray in the American version of the Church of England, as the Revolutionary War exposes divided loyalties (Anglican)
1776-1779	Many Methodist preachers and congregants, loyal to England, flee to Canada or England
1776-1783	30 Presbyterian ministers enroll in Continental Army as chaplains
1776	Three Catholics sign the Declaration of Independence (and later, the Constitution) – Thomas Fitzsimmons, Charles Carroll, and Daniel Carroll
1776	Rev. John Witherspoon, a Presbyterian minister, signs the Declaration of Independence
1783	Conference of churches in Maryland adopts the name Protestant Episcopal Church
1784	Christmas Conference in Baltimore organizes Methodist Episcopal Church and appoints first bishops – Francis Asbury and Thomas Coke

Date	Events
1789	First meeting of the House of Bishops – church constitution adopted in Philadelphia. Formal separation from the Church of England (Anglican)
1789	First General Assembly (Presbyterian)
1792	First General Conference held (Methodist)
1793	73,471 Baptists in the U.S., 25% of them Black[2]

The 1700s would see rapid growth among Protestant Churches in America, and an important new denomination – the Methodists – would set the stage for a great religious revival in the next century.

An earlier religious revival, now called the Great Awakening, was ignited by the preaching of a Calvinist Congregationalist minister named Jonathan Edwards, author of what is perhaps the most famous sermon in American history (*Sinners in the Hands of an Angry God*). The revival spread to the 13 colonies because of the charisma and speaking ability of a Calvinist Methodist preacher named George Whitefield.

The 1700s also saw the emergence of an issue that continues to split Protestantism today – the difference between Spirit-led worship and a rationalist/liturgical view. Baptists, for example, split into "Old Lights" (rationalists) and "New Lights" (more focused on the impact of the Holy Spirit and emotionalism). In 1740, the Presbyterian Church split over feuds between "new side" revivalists and "old side" Calvinists. While Calvinist/rationalist preacher Jonathan Edwards sparked the Great Awakening, he was suspicious of overt emotionalism in worship.

An even greater split impacted the 1700s, as denominations, churches, pastors, and congregants chose sides during the American Revolution.

Great Awakening

The first great revival in America started at a small church in Northhampton, Massachusetts in 1734. Calvinist preacher Jonathan Edwards preached five sermons that had a profound impact on his congregation (300 were saved in the course of a winter), and inhabitants of nearby towns. In time, the Great Awakening would impact all of New England; with the arrival of George Whitefield to the United States in 1740, it would spread to the rest of the country, and even to England.

---

[2] *Handbook of Denominations in the United States*, by Frank S. Mead and Samuel S. Hill (Abingdon, 1995)

Jonathan Edwards would later write about his experiences during the beginning of the Great Awakening in his book *A Faithful Narrative of the Surprising Work of God*:

> The work in this town, and others about us, has been extraordinary on account of the universality of it, affecting all sorts, sober and vicious, high and low, rich and poor, wise and unwise...
>
> This dispensation has also appeared very extraordinary in the numbers of those on whom we have reason to hope it has had a saving effect. We have about six hundred and twenty communicants, which include almost all our adult persons. The church was very large before; but persons never thronged into it as they did in the late extraordinary time. Our sacraments are eight weeks asunder, and I received into our communion about a hundred before one sacrament, fourscore of them at one time, whose appearance, when they presented themselves together to make an open explicit profession of Christianity, was very affecting to the congregation...
>
> I am far from pretending to be able to determine how many have lately been the subjects of such mercy; but if I may be allowed to declare any thing that appears to me probable in a thing of thin nature, I hope that **more than 300 souls were savingly brought home to Christ, in this town, in the space of half a year**, and about the same number of males as female...
>
> ...These awakenings when they have first seized on persons, have had two effects; one was, that they have brought them immediately to quit their sinful practices; and the looser sort have been brought to forsake and dread their former vices and extravagances. When once the Spirit of God began to be so wonderfully poured out in a general way through the town, people had soon done with their old quarrels, backbitings, and intermeddling with other men's matters. The tavern was soon left empty, and persons kept very much at home; none went abroad unless on necessary business, or on some religious account, and every day seemed in many respects like a Sabbath-day. The other effect was, that it put them on earnest application to the means of salvation, reading, prayer, meditation, the ordinances of God's house, and private conference; their cry was, What shall we do to be saved? **The place of resort was now altered, it was no longer the tavern, but the minister's house that was thronged far more than ever the tavern had been wont to be**.[3]

---

[3] *A Faithful Narrative of the Surprising Work of God* by Jonathan Edwards (emphasis added)

It should be noted that this revival in the beginning was not like the great revivals of the 19th Century, or Billy Graham crusades in the 20th century. As Edwards wrote above, it was the church house, not the camp meeting or stadium that was the center of the revival. There was little of the ecstatic fervor of later revivals – after all, Jonathan Edwards was a Calvinist rationalist, and would have considered the excesses of later revivals as suspicious. The beginning of the Great Awakening was characterized by people reflecting on their own sinful life, wanting to "get right" with God, seeking out others to talk to about God, and focusing on matters of church and faith on an everyday basis.

And certainly, Jonathan Edwards didn't coddle his congregations. The most famous example of his sermons (perhaps the most famous sermon ever preached in America) was the fiery *Sinners in the Hands of an Angry God* – a faithful representation of basic Calvinist principles. Some excerpts:

> There is no want of power in God to cast wicked men into hell at any moment...

> They deserve to be cast into hell; so that divine justice never stands in the way, it makes no objection against God's using his power at any moment to destroy them. Yea, on the contrary, justice calls aloud for an infinite punishment of their sins.

> They are already under a sentence of condemnation to hell...

> They are now the objects of that very same anger and wrath of God, that is expressed in the torments of hell. And the reason why they do not go down to hell at each moment, is not because God, in whose power they are, is not then very angry with them; as he is with many miserable creatures now tormented in hell, who there feel and bear the fierceness of his wrath. Yea, God is a great deal more angry with great numbers that are now on earth: yea, doubtless, with many that are now in this congregation, who it may be are at ease, than he is with many of those who are now in the flames of hell...

> The devil stands ready to fall upon them, and seize them as his own, at what moment God shall permit him. They belong to him; he has their souls in his possession, and under his dominion...

> There are in the souls of wicked men those hellish principles reigning, that would presently kindle and flame out into hell fire, if it were not for God's restraints...

God has laid himself under no obligation, by any promise to keep any natural man out of hell one moment...[4]

The Great Awakening became a national sensation under fiery Methodist/Calvinist preacher George Whitefield (pronounced "Whit-field"). According to *Christian History* magazine, "about 80% of all American colonists heard him speak at least once".[5] "In his lifetime, Whitefield preached at least 18,000 times. He addressed perhaps 10,000,000 hearers".[6]

Whitefield was born in England in 1714, and, along with Charles and John Wesley, founded the *Holy Club* at Oxford. The Holy Club had some characteristics of a lay monastic order — it was dedicated to the study of scriptures, adopted a strict moral code, encouraged periodic fasting, and had a thriving prison ministry. Out of this organization came the Methodists.

Although Whitefield was an ordained deacon in the Anglican Church (and an ordained priest by 1739), he was not welcome to preach in many churches. Like his friend John Wesley, he started preaching outdoors instead, which allowed a much larger number of people to hear him. He preached during several periods in America, the first being in 1739-1740. In 1740, he preached at Jonathan Edwards' church in Northampton, MA. He founded an orphanage in Georgia, which served as his home base during visits to America.

While Jonathan Edwards may be considered to be the theological father of the first great religious revival in the United States, George Whitefield would be its greatest celebrity.

Wesleys' Visit

Most of the early Reformers never visited America — Luther, Calvin, Zwingli, Tyndale, John Smythe, Menno Simons, etc. However, two of the founders of what would become one of the greatest Protestant denominations in the world spent two years in Georgia — John and Charles Wesley, founders of the Methodist Church.

The visit occurred between 1735-1737. As well as serving as parish priests, the Wesleys also did mission work with the local Indians. John fell in love

---

[4] *Sinners in the Hands of an Angry God*, by Jonathan Edwards (1703-1758), Enfield, Connecticut, July 8, 1741
[5] *Christian History*, Issue 38, Spring 1993
[6] *Ibid*

with a local girl, Sophy Hopkey, but was too shy to ask her to marry him. When she married another, John Wesley left Georgia in disgust, and headed back to England in a deep depression. He supposedly said on the ship home, "I went to America to convert the Indians, but, oh, who will convert me?"

Although the Wesleys didn't enjoy their visit to the new world, it would sow the seeds for future Methodists who would have an enormous impact on America (and later, the United States), including George Whitefield and Francis Asbury.

Wesley Monument at Fort Pulaski, Georgia (Photo by Robert Jones)

Revolutionary War

"The rebels of '76--Or the first announcement of the great declaration"[7]

The ideology of the American Revolution was a mixture of Calvinism and En-lightenment humanism.

On the Calvinism side, many Colonial pastors believed that one needed only be faithful to the government if the government was faithful to God. This view came directly out of Calvinist thought. Calvin believed that both Church and State were responsible to God, but felt that they should not rule over each other. He felt that Divine/Natural Law should form the foundation for all secular government, and that God establishes States to enforce Divine Laws.

Calvin believed that the populace should obey the law, unless commanded to do what is contrary to God's Law. To Calvin, unjust rulers or dictators could be removed by the populace. Calvin also believed that democratically elected officials were more likely to govern justly. A Calvinist (Presbyterian)

---

[7] Library of Congress LC-DIG-pga-03091

minister, John Witherspoon, was the only pastor to sign the Declaration of Independence.

As a sign of church support for the Revolution, more than 100 pastors served as chaplains in the Continental Army.

On the Enlightenment side, many of our nation's fathers, such as Benjamin Franklin and Thomas Jefferson, were probably Deists, as opposed to card-carrying Christians. Hence, the lack of references to Christ or Jesus in our nation's foundational documents, and the (somewhat strange to modern audiences) references to the "Creator of the Universe", "Providence", "Nature's God", etc. Their ideological influences were Enlightenment figures such as John Locke and Voltaire.

The foundational documents of the Revolution, such as the Declaration of Independence and *Common Sense*, are replete with references to God. In the Declaration of Independence, the concept of a creator God is invoked several times to justify what the Colonies were about to do. Citizens are entitled to rights from the "Law of Nature and Nature's God"; they are "endowed by their Creator with certain unalienable Rights"; the signers are "appealing to the Supreme Judge of the world for the rectitude of our intentions".

> The unanimous Declaration of the thirteen united States of America
>
> When in the Course of human events it becomes necessary for one people to dissolve the political bands which have connected them with another and to assume among the powers of the earth, the separate and equal station to which the **Laws of Nature and of Nature's God** entitle them, a decent respect to the opinions of mankind requires that they should declare the causes which impel them to the separation.
>
> We hold these truths to be self-evident, that all men are created equal, **that they are endowed by their Creator with certain unalienable Rights, that among these are Life, Liberty and the pursuit of Happiness**.
>
> We, therefore, the Representatives of the united States of America, in General Congress, Assembled, **appealing to the Supreme Judge of the world for the rectitude of our intentions**, do, in the Name, and by Authority of the good People of these Colonies, solemnly publish and declare, That these united Colonies are, and of Right ought to be Free and Independent States...**And for the support of this Declaration,**

with a firm reliance on the protection of Divine Providence, we mutually pledge to each other our Lives, our Fortunes, and our sacred Honor. (Excerpts from the Declaration of Independence, emphasis added)

In *Common Sense* by Thomas Paine, God and the Bible were invoked numerous times to make points in favor of the American Revolutionary cause. Some examples include:

- Invoking the Old Testament as proof that Kings have no moral basis
- Viewing that the distance between England and America, and the fact that America was discovered before the Reformation were divinely guided
- Viewing that the colonies should recognize only one King — "he reigns above, and does not make havoc of mankind like the Royal Brute of England"

> **Government by kings was first introduced into the world by the Heathens**, from whom the children of Israel copied the custom. It was the most prosperous invention the Devil ever set on foot for the promotion of idolatry...
>
> As the exalting one man so greatly above the rest cannot be justified on the equal rights of nature, so neither can it be defended on the authority of scripture; for **the will of the Almighty as declared by Gideon, and the prophet Samuel, expressly disapproves of government by Kings...**
>
> **Even the distance at which the Almighty hath placed England and America is a strong and natural proof that the authority of the one over the other, was never the design of Heaven.** The time likewise at which the Continent was discovered, adds weight to the argument, and the manner in which it was peopled, increases the force of it. **The Reformation was preceded by the discovery of America: As if the Almighty graciously meant to open a sanctuary to the persecuted in future years, when home should afford neither friendship nor safety.**
>
> **But where says some is the King of America? I'll tell you Friend, he reigns above, and doth not make havoc of mankind like the Royal Brute of Britain...** (*Common Sense* by Thomas Paine; emphasis added)

In Patrick Henry's famous "Give me liberty or give me death" speech in March of 1775, he invoked "an appeal to arms and to the God of hosts, and also introduced the concept that there is a "just God who presides over the destinies of nations".

> If we wish to be free...we must fight! I repeat it, sir, we must fight! **An appeal to arms and to the God of Hosts is all that is left us!**
>
> Sir, we are not weak, if we make a proper use of the means which the God of nature hath placed in our power. Three millions of people, armed in the holy cause of liberty, and in such a country as that which we possess, are invincible by any force which our enemy can send against us. Besides, sir, we shall not fight our battles alone. **There is a just God who presides over the destinies of nations, and who will raise up friends to fight our battles for us**. (Patrick Henry, March 23, 1775)

The Revolutionary War produced the first great schism within Protestantism within America, as many Anglicans continued to support England and the King, while most Calvinists supported the Revolution. In 1789, the Episcopal Church formerly separated from the Anglican church.

Chapter Three – 1800s

Date	Events
August 6, 1801	Revival at Cane Ridge, Kentucky draws 20,000 people
1816	The African Methodist Episcopal Church formed (Methodist)
1830	Boston newspaper man William Lloyd Garrison starts the abolitionist movement
1830-31	Charles Finney leads the Great Rochester Revival
1833/34	Mexican government secularizes most Roman Catholic missions in California (*An Act for the Secularization of the Missions of California*)
1837	More splits in the Presbyterian church - "Old School" vs. "New School" – over missionary expenditures, and over partnership with the Congregationalists
1844	Methodist General Conference asks a Southern Bishop to stop practicing his office as long as he remains a slaveholder
1845	Split of Methodists into Methodist Episcopal Church, Northern Body and Methodist Episcopal Church, South
1845	Southern Baptist Convention formed
1846	"New School" Presbyterians condemn slavery
1847	Missouri Synod formed (Lutheran)
1851	Anti-slavery novel *Uncle Tom's Cabin* first appears in the abolitionist newspaper *National Era*
December 2, 1859	Abolitionist John Brown is hung
1857 - 1858	"Third Great Awakening" sweeps the United States
1861 – 1865	• Protestant Episcopal Church stays intact during the Civil War • 250,000 converts to Christianity in the Union and Confederate armies
1861	United States Christian Commission formed
1861	47 "Old School" presbyteries form the Presbyterian Church in the Confederate States of America
1863	United Synod of the South created (Lutheran)
1864	"In God We Trust" first put on U.S. coins
1864	Episcopal Bishop Leonidas Polk, Lt. General, C.S.A. killed at Battle of Pine Mountain, June 14, 1864
1867	National Holiness Camp Meeting Association formed
1867	Southern churches form the Presbyterian Church in the United States (PCUS)

Date	Events
1870	"Old School" and "New School" churches reunite in the North (Presbyterian)
1890	6,231,417 Catholics in the United States[8] (Roman Catholic Church)
1895	National Baptist Convention of Americas formed, consolidating various Black Baptist groups
1896	Speaking in tongues occurs at a Holiness meeting in North Carolina (Pentecostal)

Defining movements in the 1800s in Protestantism included:
- Splits between northern and southern denominations over the issue of slavery
- The rise of the camp meeting or revival as a key form of worship (and the rise of the Holiness movement and Pentecostalism)
- The abolition and temperance movements which moved Protestantism into politics in a big way

The Great Revival

"19th Century Camp Meeting"[9]

---

[8] *Handbook of Denominations in the United States*, by Frank S. Mead and Samuel S. Hill (Abingdon, 1995)
[9] Library of Congress LC-USZC4-4554

The 1800s experienced an almost continual cycle of revivals, including the "Great Revival" of the early part of the century, the Holiness movement, revivals in the camps of Northern and Southern armies during the Civil War, and the Pentecostal movement of the latter-part of the 19th century. These revivals would prove very different from the more staid "Great Awakening" of the 18th century.

The roots of the great revival movements of the 19th century can be traced to an auspicious moment in the late-18th century – John Wesley appointed Francis Asbury as the first bishop of the Methodist church in America. Asbury would establish the prototype of the "circuit riding preacher" that would be followed for the next 100 years. Like John and Charles Wesley in England, Asbury's ministry was very mobile - he is said to have traveled 250,000 - 300,000 miles in his ministry, and preached 17,000 sermons from Maine to Georgia.[10]

The idea of a circuit riding preacher arose out of the first migrations West in the late 18th and early 19th centuries ("West", in this context, referring to Kentucky, Tennessee, etc.) In the small, isolated towns that grew up during this migration, there was rarely any formal religious establishment.

The circuit riders would travel from 200 – 500 miles on a circuit of towns that typically took 2-6 weeks. Unlike the educated pastors in the rationalist Northeast denominations (Congregationalist, Anglican/Episcopal, Presbyterian, etc.), the circuit riders were often lacking in formal education, and often focused on emotionalism over rationalism in their preaching delivery. Like the Wesleys, they would often preach early in the morning to catch the attention of people on their way to work. Often coming from working class backgrounds themselves, the circuit riders could usually "connect" better with their parishioners than a traditional church-based pastor could.

In the wild frontier areas, old mainline congregations had little influence. This allowed newer denominations such as the Baptists and Methodists (and later, the Holiness movement and Pentecostals) to grow rapidly in both numbers and influence. And all these newer denominations were more focused on Spirit-led rather than rationalist-focused worship. This set the stage for the great revivals of the early 19th Century.

The first big revival in the 1800s started on August 6, 1801 at Cane Ridge, Kentucky. The revival attracted 20,000, and set the stage for revivals

---

[10] *Christian History*, Issue 45

throughout the 19th century. Barton Stone (1772 – 1844), a local Presbyterian pastor, was a preacher at the event. He later described some of the events that occurred during this revival. Note the incorporation of overtly physical dimensions at the revival – "The Jerk", falling down as if dead, the "Running Exercise", etc. This was not their grandfathers' revival (i.e. The Great Awakening). This was a very emotion-filled and Spirit-led form of worship that had never been seen before. Stone himself uses the words "eccentricities" and "fanaticism" to describe the event.

> The bodily agitations or exercises, attending the excitement in the beginning of this century, were various, and called by various names;-- as, the falling exercise--the jerks--the dancing exercise--the barking exercise--the laughing and singing exercise, &c.--The falling exercise was very common among all classes, the saints and sinners of every age and of every grace, from the philosopher to the clown. The subject of this exercise would, generally, with a piercing scream, fall like a log on the floor, earth, or mud, and appear as dead...

> The **jerks** cannot be so easily described. Sometimes the subject of the jerks would be affected in some one member of the body, and sometimes in the whole system. When the head alone was affected, it would be jerked backward and forward, or from side to side, so quickly that the features of the face could not be distinguished. When the whole system was affected, I have seen the person stand in one place, and jerk backward and forward in quick succession, their head nearly touching the floor behind and before...Though so awful to behold, I do not remember that any one of the thousands I have seen ever sustained an injury in body. This was as strange as the exercise itself.

> The **dancing exercise**. This generally began with the jerks, and was peculiar to professors of religion. The subject, after jerking awhile, began to dance, and then the jerks would cease. Such dancing was indeed heavenly to the spectators; there was nothing in it like levity, nor calculated to excite levity in the beholders...

> The **barking exercise**, (as opposers contemptuously called it,) was nothing but the jerks. A person affected with the jerks, especially in his head, would often make a grunt, or bark, if you please, from the suddenness of the jerk...

> The **laughing exercise** was frequent, confined solely with the religious. It was a loud, hearty laughter, but one *sui generis*; it excited laughter in none else. The subject appeared rapturously solemn, and his laughter excited solemnity in saints and sinners. It is truly indescribable.

The **running exercise** was nothing more than, that persons feeling something of these bodily agitations, through fear, attempted to run away, and thus escape from them; but it commonly happened that they ran not far, before they fell, or became so greatly agitated that they could proceed no farther...

I shall close this chapter with the **singing exercise**. This is more unaccountable than any thing else I ever saw. The subject in a very happy state of mind would sing most melodiously, not from the mouth or nose, but entirely in the breast, the sounds issuing thence. Such music silenced every thing, and attracted the attention of all. It was most heavenly. None could ever be tired of hearing it.

Thus have I given a brief account of the wonderful things that happened in the great excitement in the beginning of this century. **That there were many eccentricities, and much fanaticism in this excitement, was acknowledged by its warmest advocates**; indeed it would have been a wonder, if such things had not appeared, in the circumstances of that time...[11]

Revival Movement in the "Sunny South"[12]

Charles Finney

While we typically think of Methodists as the key instigators of the early-19th century revival, "New School" Presbyterians also took a part. Perhaps the

[11] *A Short History of the Life of Barton W. Stone Written by Himself* (1847), by Barton W. Stone (emphasis added)
[12] Library of Congress LC-USZ62-117140

most famous "New School" Presbyterian was Charles Finney who, starting in 1824, began a long campaign to evangelize the Northeast. In 1830-31, he led the Great Rochester Revival.

Finney was not a "normal" Presbyterian. He believed that Christians could "will to save" themselves, seemingly rejecting predestination. He was an early proponent of the Christian perfectionism movement (later adopted by the Holiness movement), which believed that it was possible for Christians to lead sinless lives (this notion would have sent Calvin whirling dervishly in his grave). He also made use of some fairly showy props such as the use of an *anxious bench* in the front of the church, where Christians with especially deep spiritual issues could sit during a service.

In time, Finney became the leader of the "New School Presbyterians", which broke away from the "Old School Presbyterians" in 1837. Eventually, Finney became a professor at the anti-slavery Oberlin College in Ohio.

Finney is sometimes referred to as the "Father of modern revivalism", although this title might also be applied to Jonathan Edwards, George White-field, or Francis Asbury.

Holiness Movement

The Holiness movement grew out of the Spirit-filled Methodist tradition. One church denomination that came directly out of the Holiness movement is the Church of the Nazarene (1,500,000 members in 2006). The Church of the Nazarene Web site lists these as the attributes of the Wesleyan-Holiness Churches[13]:

- Born out of the 19th-century holiness revivals
- Accepted pietism emphasis
- Reemphasis on sanctification as second work
- Possibility of a sinless life
- Sanctification both instantaneous and progressive
- Revival oriented
- Missionary minded
- Simple worship
- Conservative in theology
- Emphasis on personal ethics

---

[13] http://www.nazarene.org/archives/history/tree.pdf

Note the "possibility of a sinless life" bullet – a view also espoused by Charles Finney.

Civil War

In our present differences, is either party without faith of being in the right? If the Almighty Ruler of Nations, with His eternal truth and justice, be on your side of the North, or on yours of the South, that truth and that justice will surely prevail by the judgment of this great tribunal of the American people. (Lincoln's First Inaugural Address, March 4, 1861)

The Civil War was a war fought over differing interpretations of the Bible – the South believed that the Bible supported slavery, the Northern abolitionists believed that it did not. Over 600,000 Americans would die over this difference in interpretation.

Both sides in the Civil War believed that they had "God on their side". Lincoln addressed this phenomenon in both of his inaugural addresses. In the Second Inaugural Address, he looked back on the great conflict, and pointed out that "The prayers of both [sides] could not be answered. That of neither has been answered fully."

> **Both read the same Bible and pray to the same God, and each invokes His aid against the other**. It may seem strange that any men should dare to ask a just God's assistance in wringing their bread from the sweat of other men's faces, but let us judge not, that we be not judged. **The prayers of both could not be answered. That of neither has been answered fully. The Almighty has His own purposes**...
>
> With malice toward none, with charity for all, **with firmness in the right as God gives us to see the right**, let us strive on to finish the work we are in, to bind up the nation's wounds, to care for him who shall have borne the battle and for his widow and his orphan, to do all which may achieve and cherish a just and lasting peace among ourselves and with all nations. (Lincoln Second Inaugural Address, March 4, 1865)

Northern churches typically took a "big picture" or symbolic view of the Bible, and believed that the Beatitudes, Christ message of "do unto others as you would have them do unto you", and the egalitarianism of the early church pointed to slavery being morally wrong. Southerners took a more literal view of the Bible, and found no direct injunctions against slavery in the scriptures. In the Old Testament, Abraham held slaves (Genesis 21: 9-10), the 10 Commandments mention slavery without speaking out against it, and

Joseph's bothers sold him into slavery. In the New Testament, Paul tells slaves to be obedient to their masters (Ephesians 6:5-8).

Abolition Movement

William Lloyd Garrison[14]

The Abolitionist movement started as early as 1830, with Boston newspaper man William Lloyd Garrison and Northeastern Quakers taking an early role. Garrison published an abolitionist newspaper named *The Liberator*, which acted as a focal point for the abolitionist cause. By 1833, the American Anti-Slavery Society was formed. The movement existed primarily in the North – Northern abolitionist tracts were often prevented from being distributed in the South.

Another prominent abolitionist was Harriet Beecher Stowe (1811 - 1896), the 7th child of revivalist Lyman Beecher. Her anti-slavery novel *Uncle Tom's Cabin* first appeared in 1851 in the abolitionist newspaper *National Era*. It

---

[14] Library of Congress LC-USZ62-10320

would sell 1,000,000 copies before the Civil War, and helped turn mass Northern opinion against slavery.

One of the more radical abolitionists was John Brown (1800 - 1859). In 1855, well into middle age, Brown led a raid on pro-slavery settlers in Pottawatomie, Kansas, and killed five. On October 16, 1859, Brown seized the government arsenal at Harper's Ferry, VA, and held it for over a day. His goal was to start a slave revolt by providing slaves with firearms. He was eventually defeated and captured by forces led by Colonel Robert E. Lee. Brown was hung on December 2, 1859, but his efforts would eventually light the flames that would result in the Civil War.

John Brown, c. 1859[15]

Finally, the great musical anthem of the North, *the Battle Hymn of the Republic*, contained an obvious reference to the abolitionist cause:

> In the beauty of the lilies Christ was born across the sea,
> With a glory in His bosom that transfigures you and me:

[15] Library of Congress LC-USZ62-89569

As He died to make men holy, let us die to make men free,
While God is marching on. (emphasis added)

The hymn was written by Julia Ward Howe (1819 - 1910), and published in 1862 in the *Atlantic Monthly*. It was set to the tune of *John Brown's Body is a Molderin' in the Grave*, and became increasingly popular throughout the war, and after the war. Much of the imagery in the song is based on the book of *Revelation* in the New Testament.

Splits Over Slavery

Differing opinions on slavery seriously impacted some Protestant denominations. In 1845, the Methodist church split into the Methodist Episcopal Church, Northern Body and Methodist Episcopal Church. In 1846, "New School" Presbyterians condemned slavery, and in 1861, 47 "Old School" presbyteries formed the Presbyterian Church in the Confederate States of America. After the War, in 1867, Southern churches formed the Presbyterian Church in the United States (PCUS). The northern and southern Presbyterian churches would not reunite until 1983.

United States Christian Commission

"Washington, District of Columbia. Group in front of Christian Commission storehouse" (1865)[16]

The U.S. Christian Commission was formed in 1861 after the First Battle of Bull Run by the YMCA and Protestant ministers. It had quasi governmental authority, and it attended to the recreational, social, and spiritual needs of

[16] Library of Congress LC-DIG-cwpb-04358

men in the Union Army. The USCC distributed 30 million religious tracts during the war.

The Great Leaders

Prayer in "Stonewall" Jackson's camp[17]

Unlike the Revolutionary War, where many of the leaders were Deists, leaders in the Civil War were often overtly Christian (and Protestant). On the Southern side, Robert E. Lee and Stonewall Jackson were both known for their piety and attendance at chaplain-delivered church services during the War.

George McClellan – one-time commander of the Union Army - ordered that the Sabbath be observed in Union army. Generals on both sides were often hesitant to fight battles on Sundays.

The religious views of Abraham Lincoln are a little harder to pin down. He often peppered his speeches with overt Christian phrases and imagery, such as this quote from his First Inaugural Address:

> Intelligence, patriotism, **Christianity, and a firm reliance on Him who has never yet forsaken this favored land** are still competent to adjust in the best way all our present difficulty. (Lincoln's First Inaugural Address, March 4, 1861)

[17] Library of Congress LC-USZ62

However, Lincoln was never closely associated with any church or denomination. After his death, he was often pictured by his admirers as a martyr to the cause, who had shed his blood to save the nation.

Revival in the Camps

Just as revivals had swept through he United States before the Civil War, revivals swept through the Confederate and Union armies at various points during the War. *Christian History* magazine estimates that 100,000 – 200,000 converts were made in the Union Army during the course of the War, and that 150,000 converts were made in the Confederate Army. In the Fall of 1863 alone, 7,000 soldiers in Lee's army were converted.[18]

Before Sherman's Atlanta Campaign started in May 1864, Union soldiers were baptized in the Chickamauga Creek near Sherman's staging area at Ringgold, GA. During the Atlanta Campaign, Confederate General John Bell Hood was baptized by Bishop (and General) Leonidas Polk on their way to the great battle at Resaca.

Results

The impact on Protestantism of the Civil War is still reverberating today. Partly because of the success of the abolitionist movement in Northern churches, Northern churches and denominations became more and more focused on a Social Gospel, and less focused on the Bible as the revealed revelation of God, and the saving grace of Christ as the Divine Son of God. Southern churches, in general, went exactly the opposite way, focusing more and more on the Bible as the revealed revelation of God and salvation as the key messages of the Bible. These differing views would continue to cause friction in the late-20th Century and early 21st. Using the Presbyterian Church as an example, after the Northern and Southern churches reunited in 1983, the next 25 years would be an almost endless struggle between the Southern Evangelical faction of the church and the liberal (modernist) northern faction of the church.

After the Civil War, Protestantism and revivalism continued their march westward. A Protestant movement that would breathe new life into both Evangelicalism and Fundamentalism would arise at the very end of the century, called Pentecostalism.

---

[18] *Christian History,* Issue 33, 1992

Chapter Four – 1900s

Date	Events
1900	Charles Fox Parham opens a Bible school in Topeka, Kansas
1901	Speaking in tongues occurs at a Holiness meeting in Topeka, Kansas
1903	A revival in Galena, Kansas gains thousands of converts to Charles Parham's message
1906	The Azusa Street Revival in Los Angeles, led by William J. Seymour becomes the foundation of the modern Pentecostal movement
1908	The Methodist Episcopal Church adopts a Social Creed at its General Conference
1910	Presbyterian General Assembly publishes Evangelical "The Five Point Deliverance"
1913	4,000,000 Methodists[19]
1914	First General Counsel of the Assemblies of God; receives ordained women into fellowship
1918	North and South reunite in United Lutheran Church
Post World War I	Methodist church strongly supports temperance movement
January 29, 1919	18th amendment to the Constitution ratified, starting Prohibition
1919	World's Christian Fundamentals Association formed
1919	Aimee Semple McPherson becomes a national sensation as a Pentecostal revivalist
1925	Scopes Monkey Trial
1926	Aimee Semple McPherson somewhat discredited in what may have been a phony kidnapping
1931	Women admitted to role of Ruling Elder (Presbyterian)
1933	Prohibition repealed
1933	Henrietta Mears founds Gospel Light Press, originally focused on Sunday School curriculum
1938	Methodist Episcopal Church, Northern Body and Methodist Episcopal Church, South reunite
1939	7.7 million Methodists after unification[20]
1941	Fundamentalist Carl McIntire founds American Council of Christian Churches
1941	Young Life is founded by Jim Rayburn

---

[19] http://archives.umc.org/interior.asp?mid=1215
[20] *Ibid*

Date	Events
1942	Harold John Ockenga forms National Association of Evangelicals
1943	Pentecostal churches join the National Association of Evangelicals
1945	Fledgling Youth for Christ movement attracts 70,000 people to Chicago's Soldier Field on Memorial Day
1950	Billy Graham show "The Hour of Decision" begins – it would eventually be broadcast on 1,000 stations nationwide
1950	Founding of Billy Graham Evangelistic Association (BGEA)
1954	Billy Graham crusade in London draws 2,000,000(!)
1956	Billy Graham co-founds *Christianity Today*
1956	Women accepted into the clergy (Methodist)
1957	Women admitted to the clergy – none were actually ordained until 1965 (Presbyterian)
1957	Many Fundamentalists break from Billy Graham because of his ecumenicalism and support for desegregation
1958	Merger of Northern churches forms United Presbyterian Church in the U.S.A.
1960	John Kennedy becomes first (and only) Catholic President
1960	Christian Broadcast Network started by Pat Robertson
1967	Confession of 1967 passed in the UPCUSA (Presbyterian)
April 23, 1968	The United Methodist Church was created, bringing together The Evangelical United Brethren Church and The Methodist Church. The new UMC had 11,000,000 members[21]
1970	Elizabeth Platz becomes the first female Lutheran pastor in North America
1970	Ordination of women as deacons approved (Anglican)
1971	*Sojourners* magazine started, an Evangelical magazine focused on social causes
1973	Trinity Broadcasting Network founded by Paul Crouch, Jan Crouch, Jim Bakker, and Tammy Bakker
1976	Prison Fellowship Ministries founded by Chuck Colson
1976	Ordination of women as priests approved (Anglican)
1976	Newsweek declares 1976 the *Year of the Evangelical*
1976	"Born again" Georgian Jimmy Carter elected to the presidency
1977	"Focus on the Family" started by James Dobson
1979	Fundamentalist pastor Jerry Falwell founds the Moral Majority
1980	Marjorie Matthews becomes first female Methodist bish-

---

[21] *Ibid*

Date	Events
	op
June 10, 1983	United Presbyterian Church in the U.S.A. and the Presbyterian Church in the United States reunite (North and South). 3,1666,050 members[22]
1984	Reverend Jesse Jackson runs for president in the Democratic primary
1987	Pat Robertson founds the Christian Coalition
1988	Reverend Jesse Jackson and Pastor Pat Robertson run for president in the Democrat and Republican primaries (respectively); Jackson wins 11 states/primaries
1992	April Ulring Larson becomes first woman Lutheran bishop in America
1994	13 million Methodists in the U.S.; 18 million around the world[23] (Methodist)
1994	32 million Baptists in 27 denominations in the U.S.[24]
1994	Episcopal Church - 2,471,880 members[25]
1998	Largest church in the world is the Yoido Full Gospel Church in Korea – 240,000 attend weekly worship[26] (Pentecostal)

The 20th century would see a continued split in Protestantism between the modernists in the mainline churches, and the Evangelical and Fundamentalist members of denominations such as the Southern Baptists and the Pentecostals. In the 1920s, the Scopes Monkey Trial led many people to believe that Fundamentalism had been discredited. In fact, it simply went underground. It would re-emerge in the second half of the 20th century in a spectacular way, using the new medium of television to spread its word.

Old style 19th century revival preachers would still be popular in the 20th century, with Billy Sunday in the first half of the 20th century, and Billy Graham and others in the second half of the 20th century.

---

[22] *Handbook of Denominations in the United States*, by Frank S. Mead and Samuel S. Hill (Abingdon, 1995)

[23] *Ibid*

[24] *Ibid*

[25] *Handbook of Denominations in the United States*, by Frank S. Mead and Samuel S. Hill (Abingdon, 1995)

[26] *Christian History*, Issue 58, 1998

Billy Sunday (1862 - 1935)

Billy Sunday, evangelist[27]

Billy Sunday was a popular baseball player from 1883-1890 with the Chicago White Sox, Philadelphia Phillies, and Pittsburgh Pirates (lifetime average: . 248, with 246+ stolen bases). In 1890, he left baseball and eventually became the most famous and influential evangelist of his time.

Sunday was converted in 1886 or 1887 after hearing a street preacher in Chicago, and attending a small mission church. Starting in 1896, he preached on the so-called "Kerosene Circuit" (i.e. cities without electricity) in Iowa and Illinois for 12 years. He started out preaching in tents, but eventually went on to preach in stadiums, and large, temporary "tabernacles".

After leaving the "Kerosene Circuit", he started preaching in small cities, and eventually in the largest cities in America. In the first two decades of the

---

[27] Library of Congress LC-B2- 1222-16[P&P]

20th century, he was one of the most famous people in America, and one of the most influential religious leaders. According to Wikipedia, he preached to more than 100 million people, preached 20,000 sermons, and saved over 1 million people in altar calls.[28]

Sunday was Evangelical, Fundamentalist, generally Calvinist, eschatological, and non-denominational (although ordained as an elder). He was a strong supporter of Prohibition, and was opposed to eugenics and the teaching of evolution.

In many ways, Sunday was the forerunner of an even more popular and influential Evangelical movement of the later 20th century – the Billy Graham Crusades. Sunday, like the later Graham, would preach an Evangelical message to large groups of people in large venues, would distribute tracts on salvation, conducted large-scale altar calls ("hit the sawdust trail"), and hobnobbed with Presidents (Wilson, T. Roosevelt, Herbert Hoover).

Scopes Monkey Trial

In 1925, the State of Tennessee passed a law making it illegal to teach evolution in a public school.

> "That it shall be unlawful for any teacher in any of the Universities, Normals and all other public schools of the State which are supported in whole or in part by the public school funds of the State, to teach any theory that denies the Story of the Divine Creation of man as taught in the Bible, and to teach instead that man has descended from a lower order of animals." (Butler Bill)

On July 10, 1925, in the sleepy little town of Dayton, TN (population 2,000), a high school teacher named John Thomas Scopes was put on trial for teaching evolution. He had clearly violated the Butler Bill, and in the 8-day trial was found guilty of a misdemeanor, and fined $100. However, the trial had a much greater impact symbolically as it became a battle between a well-known Fundamentalist and a well-known agnostic. The Fundamentalist, who acted for the prosecution, was William Jennings Bryan, a three-time Democratic Presidential Candidate (1896, 1900 and 1908). The agnostic, Clarence Darrow, acted for the defense. Darrow had a reputation for supporting "radicals".

---

[28] www.wikipedia.org

William Jennings Bryan[29]

The most famous part of the trial occurred when Clarence Darrow asked to put Bryan on the stand. This highly unusual move had to be approved by both Bryan and Judge John Raulston. The questioning of Bryan by Darrow had nothing to do with the guilt or innocence of John Scopes, but rather was an attempted attack on Fundamentalist beliefs. Darrow examined Bryan on issues such as the age of the earth, whether the earth was created in 6 days, whether the story of Jonah and the whale should be taken literally, where Cain's wife came from, and the nature of the serpent in the book of Genesis. Some excerpts follow.

Examination of W.J. Bryan by Clarence Darrow, of counsel for the defense:

Q--You claim that everything in the Bible should be literally interpreted?

A--I believe everything in the Bible should be accepted as it is given there: some of the Bible is given illustratively. For instance: "Ye are

---

[29] Library of Congress LC-USZ62-95709

the salt of the earth." I would not insist that man was actually salt, or that he had flesh of salt, but it is used in the sense of salt as saving God's people.

Q--But when you read that Jonah swallowed the whale--or that the whale swallowed Jonah-- excuse me please--how do you literally interpret that?

A--When I read that a big fish swallowed Jonah--it does not say whale....That is my recollection of it. A big fish, and I believe it, and I believe in a God who can make a whale and can make a man and make both what He pleases...

Bryan--Your honor, they have not asked a question legally and the only reason they have asked any question is for the purpose, as the question about Jonah was asked, for a chance to give this agnostic an opportunity to criticize a believer in the world of God; and I answered the question in order to shut his mouth so that he cannot go out and tell his atheistic friends that I would not answer his questions. That is the only reason, no more reason in the world. ..

Mr. Darrow:

Q--Mr. Bryan, do you believe that the first woman was Eve?

A--Yes.

Q--Do you believe she was literally made out of Adams's rib?

A--I do.

Q--Did you ever discover where Cain got his wife?

A--No, sir; I leave the agnostics to hunt for her...

Q--The Bible says he got one, doesn't it? Were there other people on the earth at that time?

A--I cannot say.

Q--You cannot say. Did that ever enter your consideration?

A--Never bothered me.

Q--There were no others recorded, but Cain got a wife.

A--That is what the Bible says.

Q--Where she came from you do not know. All right. Does the statement, "The morning and the evening were the first day," and "The morning and the evening were the second day," mean anything to you?

A-- I do not think it necessarily means a twenty-four-hour day.

Q--You do not?

A--No.

Q--What do you consider it to be?

A--I have not attempted to explain it. If you will take the second chapter--let me have the book. (Examining Bible.) The fourth verse of the second chapter says: "These are the generations of the heavens and of the earth, when they were created in the day that the Lord God made the earth and the heavens," the word "day" there in the very next chapter is used to describe a period. I do not see that there is any necessity for construing the words, "the evening and the morning," as meaning necessarily a twenty-four-hour day, "in the day when the Lord made the heaven and the earth."

Q--Then, when the Bible said, for instance, "and God called the firmament heaven. And the evening and the morning were the second day," that does not necessarily mean twenty-four hours?

A--I do not think it necessarily does.[30]

Both sides represented large swaths of belief systems in the country at the time, and each side couldn't understand how the other side could hold the beliefs that they did. (Several times during the trial, Clarence Darrow referred to Fundamentalists as "ignoramuses"). The liberal side of Protestantism assumed that in time, as science "proved" conservative Christianity to be wrong, that more and more Christians would become liberals. They thought it was amusing that there were Christians in 1925 that thought that the world was only 6,000 years old. Fundamentalist Christians were astonished that liberals could believe in such an unproven philosophy as evolution that viewed that, ultimately, humans had evolved spontaneously from some sort of primordial ooze.

---

[30] http://www.law.umkc.edu/faculty/projects/ftrials/scopes/scopes2.htm

Clarence Darrow[31]

The Scopes "Monkey Trial" has traditionally been positioned as a great defeat for Fundamentalists, as much of the mainstream press ridiculed Fundamentalist beliefs. However, I strongly disagree with this view. The Scopes trial took widely disparate groups of Fundamentalists and turned them into a movement. Although they would later break with him, Fundamentalists would be an initial audience for Billy Graham, and, along with the broader Evangelical movement in the late 20th century and early 21st century, would elect 7 Republicans to the presidency in a space of 28 years.

What the Scopes Monkey Trial *did* do, though, was to underscore a widening gulf in American Protestantism that had been simmering since the Civil War. Northeastern, mainline Christianity was becoming increasingly liberal theologically and increasingly focused on a Social Gospel. Evangelical Christianity mostly centered in the South and Midwest turned increasingly towards a conservative theological position. These two broad frameworks for Protestantism would never come together again, and remain as starkly opposed in 2010 as they were in 1925.

[31] Library of Congress LC-USZ62-11819

Prohibition and the Temperance Movement

There had been temperance movements in the United States since the 1700s, but they really began to pick up steam in the late 19th and early 20th centuries. In 1880s, the Women's Christian Temperance Union started a massive education effort on the evils of alcoholism. In the past, such efforts had only limited impact on a nation that liked its liquor. By the 1880s, though, several factors combined to make the message more compelling – the health risks of alcoholism were becoming clearer, the tendency to create broken homes had been noted, the connection between alcoholism and absenteeism in the nascent industrial revolution were becoming apparent, and the burgeoning women's movement associated alcoholism with domestic violence.

"Woman's Holy War – Grand Charge on the Enemy's Works"[32]

Perhaps the most famous temperance advocate (Susan B. Anthony was another) was Carrie A. Nation (1846 – 1911), who became famous for busting up taverns with a hatchet. She got her start in Kansas when she started a

[32] Library of Congress LC-USZ62-683

45

branch of the Women's Christian Temperance Union, and went around the countryside lecturing to tavern owners on the evils of alcohol. Starting in 1900, Carrie Nation started vandalizing bars, first with rocks, and later with a hatchet. Often arrested, her fame spread throughout the country.

Carrie Nation[33]

The apogee and greatest success of the Temperance Movement happened after World War I with the passage of the 18th amendment to the Constitution, and the passing of the Volstad Act. Prohibition had started.

> Section 1. After one year from the ratification of this article the manufacture, sale, or transportation of intoxicating liquors within, the importation thereof into, or the exportation thereof from the United States and all territory subject to the jurisdiction thereof for beverage purposes is hereby prohibited.
>
> Section 2. The Congress and the several States shall have concurrent power to enforce this article by appropriate legislation.

---

[33] Library of Congress LC-DIG-ggbain-05640

Section 3. This article shall be inoperative unless it shall have been ratified as an amendment to the Constitution by the legislatures of the several States, as provided in the Constitution, within seven years from the date of the submission hereof to the States by the Congress. (18th amendment to the Constitution, ratified January 29, 1919)

TITLE II.

PROHIBITION OF INTOXICATING BEVERAGES.

SEC. 3. No person shall on or after the date when the eighteenth amendment to the Constitution of the United States goes into effect, manufacture, sell, barter, transport import, export, deliver, furnish or possess any intoxicating liquor except as authorized in this Act, and all the provisions of this Act shall be liberally construed to the end that the use of intoxicating liquor as a beverage may be prevented. (Volstad Act)

There were medical and sacramental exceptions to the Volstad Act, but in general, use of liquor in the United States had been outlawed. The Act and amendment were repealed in 1933.

Today it is popular to ridicule Prohibition, or to blame the rise of organized crime in America on "those meddling women". But in 2010, alcoholism continues to take a huge toll on America.

Ninety five percent of alcoholics die of their disease, approximately 26 years earlier than their normal life expectancy. Heavy drinking contributes to illnesses in each of the top three causes of death: heart disease, cancer and stroke. Approximately two-thirds of American adults drink an alcoholic beverage during the course of a year, and at least 13.8 million Americans develop problems associated with drinking. Fifty percent of cases involving major trauma are alcohol related. Fifty percent of homicides are alcohol related. Forty percent of assaults are alcohol related. One hundred thousand Americans die of alcohol problems each year. More than 40% of those who start drinking at age 14 or younger become alcoholic. In 1998, the cost of alcohol abuse was over 185 billion dollars.[34]

Today, many people associate anti-alcohol campaigns with the religious right, but at the time, the temperance movement was considered a "pro-

---

[34] http://www.robertperkinson.com/alcoholism_statistics.htm

gressive" (liberal) cause, since alcoholism so negatively impacted the poor and women.

Rise of "New Evangelicalism"

Rev. Billy Graham[35]

Evangelicalism and Fundamentalism as we know them today were being formed in the mid-20th century in "parachurch" organizations, not linked to a specific denomination. An early example might be in 1933 when Henrietta Mears founded Gospel Light Press, originally focused on Sunday School curriculum. Other Evangelical and Fundamentalist parachurch organizations would be formed in rapid succession:

- 1941 – Young Life founded by Jim Rayburn
- 1941 - Fundamentalist Carl McIntire founds American Council of Christian Churches
- 1942 - Harold John Ockenga forms National Association of Evangelicals
- July 22, 1945 – Founding of Youth for Christ International

---

[35] Library of Congress LC-U9- 15743-7 [P&P]

The two latter organizations would be especially important, as they formed the home base of a young Evangelical preacher named Billy Graham.

The existence of both the Fundamentalist American Council of Christian Churches and the Evangelical National Association of Evangelicals shows an early division in conservative theological ranks. Ockenga coined the term "New Evangelicalism" to describe his nascent movement. New Evangelicals:

- Believed in the authority (although not necessarily the inerrancy) of the Bible
- Believed in the importance of a conversion experience
- Believed that salvation could only come through Christ
- Believed in the ancient Christian Creeds

However, the New Evangelicals were not anti-intellectual, anti-science, or separationist (from the broader secular society). As such, New Evangelicals are often viewed as being between positioned somewhere between modernism/neo-orthodoxy and Fundamentalism.

When the Youth for Christ International organization was founded in July 1945, it hired a young Southern Baptist preacher named Billy Graham. Over the next year, Graham would preach in 47 of 48 states.

Graham's career would really take off in 1949 during the Greater Los Angeles Revival. A now-famous memo from William Randolph Hearst was sent to reporters and newspapers around the country that said "puff Graham" ("puff" as in "play up someone in a favorable way"). Graham would soon be known throughout the United States and throughout the world as the most prominent Protestant preacher. In 1954, the Billy Graham Crusade in London drew 2,000,000(!) people.

The New York Crusade in 1957 would be an auspicious one for the future of Evangelicalism for two reasons. First, Evangelicals would use a new medium to spread their message when ABC televised the Billy Graham Crusade. Secondly, Billy Graham would speak out against segregation, and on one evening, he invited Dr. Martin Luther King, Jr. to join him on the stage. Graham also extended a hand of Fellowship to Roman Catholics. As a result, many Fundamentalists split from Billy Graham's ministry, and the terms Evangelical and Fundamentalist came to no longer be used synonymously.

However, the New York Crusade, which ran Memorial Day to Labor Day, was a huge success, with attendance of 2,000,000.

Billy Graham is also known as the "preacher to presidents". Graham has had close relationships with every president since (and including) Dwight Eisenhower.

A good way of judging the impact of Billy Graham is through the number of people that he has reached in his ministry. According to Wikipedia:

> Graham has preached in person to more people around the world than any protestant who has ever lived. As of 1993, more than 2.5 million people had stepped forward at his crusades to "accept Jesus Christ as their personal saviour." As of 2002, Graham's lifetime audience, including radio and television broadcasts, topped two billion.[36]

Religion and Politics

Like the earlier abolition and temperance movements, Protestantism and politics would mix throughout the 20th century, especially in the 2nd half of the century. Much of the Civil Rights movement in the 1950s and 1960s was driven from black churches, and prominent black clergymen were key leaders, including Dr. Martin Luther King, Rev. Jesse Jackson, and Rev. Ralph David Abernathy, Jr. Martin Luther King's famous "I have a Dream Speech" was specifically focused on the passage of the federal Civil Rights legislation, and contained unabashed Christian imagery.

> I have a dream that one day every valley shall be exalted, every hill and mountain shall be made low, the rough places will be made plain, and the crooked places will be made straight, and the glory of the Lord shall be revealed, and all flesh shall see it together...

> And when this happens, when we allow freedom to ring, when we let it ring from every village and every hamlet, from every state and every city, we will be able to speed up that day when all of God's children, black men and white men, Jews and Gentiles, Protestants and Catholics, will be able to join hands and sing in the words of the old Negro spiritual, "Free at last! free at last! thank God Almighty, we are free at last!"[37]

---

[36] http://www.wikipedia.org/
[37] "I Have a Dream" speech, by Dr. Martin Luther King Jr., August 28, 1963, Lincoln Memorial

In 1976, Jimmy Carter (a member of the Southern Baptist Convention until 2000) became the first President who claimed to be "born again". He would not be the last. The phrase confused the press for a period, as they obviously had never heard of the concept before, even though something like 65 million Americans considered themselves to be Evangelicals at the time.

In 1984 and 1988, Rev. Jesse Jackson ran for the presidency in the Democratic primary. According to Wikipedia:

> Jackson garnered 3,282,431 primary votes, or 18.2 percent of the total, in 1984, and won five primaries and caucuses, including Louisiana, the District of Columbia, South Carolina, Virginia, and one of two separate contests in Mississippi.[38]

In 1988, Jackson ran again in the Democratic primary, and mounted an even stronger campaign than in 1984:

> He captured 6.9 million votes and won 11 contests; seven primaries (Alabama, the District of Columbia, Georgia, Louisiana, Mississippi, Puerto Rico and Virginia) and four caucuses (Delaware, Michigan, South Carolina and Vermont). Jackson also scored March victories in Alaska's caucuses and Texas's local conventions, despite losing the Texas primary. Some news accounts credit him with 13 wins. Briefly, after he won 55% of the vote in the Michigan Democratic caucus, he was considered the frontrunner for the nomination, as he surpassed all the other candidates in total number of pledged delegates.[39]

White Evangelicals would also enter the political fray in a big way. Protestant Evangelicals are often credited with the two landslide elections of Ronald Reagan in the 1980s. And in 1988, one of the most prominent white Evangelical pastors, Pat Robertson, ran for president in the Republican primary. Robertson finished second in the Iowa caucus, and won the Washington caucus. He eventually dropped out of the primary, and supported George H.W. Bush at the 1988 Republican convention. Robertson would go on to found the Christian Coalition.

The Christian Coalition was founded by Pat Robertson in 1987, but didn't become active until after Robertson's failed run for the presidency in 1988. The initial focus was on encouraging the nation's 65 million Evangelical

---

[38] http://www.wikipedia.org/
[39] Ibid

voters to get out and vote. In time, the Christian Coalition became involved in other matters, such as providing legal help to Christians who felt they had been discriminated against because of their religious beliefs. Ralph Reed ran the Christian Coalition starting in 1989.

Evangelicals and the Media

As already mentioned, major television networks started broadcasting Billy Graham Crusades as early as 1957. In 1960, Pat Robertson started CBN, the Christian Broadcast Network. In time, his show *700 Club* would become an important media outlet for Evangelicals.

In 1973, Paul Crouch, Jan Crouch, Jim Bakker, and Tammy Bakker started the Trinity Broadcast Network, which is one of the most popular networks on television today. The Bakkers would leave soon to start their PTL (Praise the Lord) network, which faltered in the late 1980s when Jim Bakker was convicted on multiple counts of mail fraud and wire fraud.

The Mainstream media has often been tone-deaf about the needs and concerns of Evangelicals. One example already cited, is the press being confused about the term "Born Again" when Jimmy Carter was running for President in 1976. Another example was in the Presidential debates in October 1984 (Reagan-Mondale). Reagan was grilled about whether he had a literal belief in the end times chapters at the end of Revelation. When he answered that he did, the press thought it was a "gotcha" moment, figuring that no one would want to vote for a President who believed in an eschatology conflagration. In fact, Evangelicals turned out in droves to vote for Reagan, providing him with the biggest landslide in American history (Electoral votes: Reagan (525); Mondale (13)).

Role of Women

Neither mainline denominations nor Evangelicals were quick to endorse women pastors/bishops/deacons/elders. The Presbyterian Church (U.S.A.) for example, didn't recognize women pastors and elders until the 1950s/60s:

> "The first ordination of women as elders in this denomination [Presbyterian Church (U.S.A.)] actually occurred in 1962. As ministers, women were ordained beginning 1965."[40]

The United Methodist Church took a similar path:

---

[40] http://www.pcusa.org/pcusa/info/women.htm

"Full clergy rights for women were finally granted in 1956, but it took a decade more before the number of women in seminaries and pulpits began to grow significantly. When Methodists and the Evangelical United Brethren united in 1968, the right of women to full clergy status was included in the plan of union."[41]

The Lutheran (1970s), Episcopal (1976) and Anglican (1992) denominations took even longer to ordain women pastors/priests.

The Southern Baptist Convention, on the other hand, recently upheld its long-standing prohibition on female pastors:

"A New Testament church of the Lord Jesus Christ is an autonomous local congregation of baptized believers, associated by covenant in the faith and fellowship of the gospel…Its scriptural officers are pastors and deacons. While both men and women are gifted for service in the church, the office of pastor is limited to men as qualified by Scripture." (Adopted by the Southern Baptist Convention June 14, 2000)[42]

Individual Baptist churches have occasionally ordained female pastors, including First Baptist Church in Marietta, GA, which ordained Lynn Swanson Fowler in 2005.

Early Pentecostals accepted women as pastors, but the typical modern practice is to forbid female pastors.

Rise of the Megachurch, and the Non-Denominational Church

As Evangelicalism rose in prominence, so did new styles of churches and new styles of worship. The 1980s and 1990s saw the rise of the megachurch, usually defined as a church with over 2,000 (sometimes 4,000) members. As the chart below shows, the megachurch phenomenon is primarily an Evangelical/Fundamentalist structure. Only 5% of megachurches are described as "Traditional". Megachurches typically have huge sanctuaries, often with theater seating. They typically have sophisticated sound systems, and feature electric guitar/drum-driven music, rather than traditional hymns.

---

[41] http://www.umc.org/churchlibrary/discipline/history/movement_toward_union.htm

[42] http://www.utm.edu/martinarea/fbc/bfm/6.html

By theology[43]:

Evangelical	56%
Charismatic	8%
Pentecostal	8%
Moderate	7%
Traditional	5%
Seeker	7%
Fundamentalist	2%
Other	7%

By denomination[44]

Nondenominational	34%
Southern Baptist	16%
Baptist unspecified	10%
Assemblies of God	6%
United Methodist	5%
Calvary Chapel	4.4%
Christian	4.2%

The rise of nondenominational churches has coincided with the rise of the megachurch in the last couple of decades. However, most nondenominational churches are Baptist or Pentecostal under the covers.

---

[43] http://hirr.hartsem.edu/megachurch/definition.html
[44] Ibid

Chapter Five – 2000s

Date	Events
2000	"Born again" George W. Bush elected President of the United States
2000	Southern Baptist Convention upholds its long-standing prohibition on female pastors
2002	Catholic Church has 66,407,105 members in the United States, making it the largest denomination in the U.S.A.[45]
2003	"The United Methodist Church has about 8.3 million members in the United States and 1.5 million members in Europe, Africa and the Philippines."[46] (Methodist)
2006	Evangelical Lutheran Church has 4,930,429 members[47] (Lutheran)
2006	Missouri Synod has 2,463,747 members[48] (Lutheran)
2006	Assemblies of God has 12,100 churches in the U.S.; 236,022 churches and outstations in 191 other nations[49] (Pentecostal)
2006	"The church has a membership of 2,405,311 in all fifty states and Puerto Rico. Presently there are 11,064 congregations, 21,194 ordained ministers, 894 candidates for ministry, and 101,324 elders."[50] (Presbyterian)
2006	The UCC has "6,500 congregations with approximately 1,800,000 members"[51] (United Church of Christ)
2008	Former Baptist preacher Mike Huckabee finishes 2nd in Republican primary for President, winning Iowa, West Virginia, Kansas, Alabama, Arkansas, Georgia, Tennessee and Louisiana

[45] http://www.adherents.com/rel_USA.html#2004total
[46] *Membership*, 5/3/2003, United Methodist Church Archives
[47] http://www.elca.org/communication/quick.html
[48] http://www.lcms.org/pages/internal.asp?NavID=2436
[49] http://ag.org/top/about/history.cfm
[50] http://www.pcusa.org/101/101-whoare.htm
[51] http://www.ucc.org/aboutus/shortcourse/early.html

As Protestantism has moved into the 21st century, the divisions that came into place during and after the Civil War that pitted Northern mainline liberal denominations against Southern and Midwestern Evangelical congregations have, if anything, sharpened. Mainline denominations have almost all been taken over by modernists (liberal; Social Gospel), and continue to lose membership. Large Baptist, Pentecostal and nondenominational Evangelical churches continue to thrive (although the Southern Baptist Convention recently reported a small down-tick in membership).

Many mainline liberal churches are discovering that in an age of secular and governmental charity programs, a Social Gospel becomes a poor (sole) *raison d'etre*. The government takes care of welfare, right?

Many Evangelicals, especially younger ones, are more focused today on social issues than in the past (although with the same core religious beliefs). Concern about the environment and helping one's fellow man is more important to many young Evangelicals than focusing on issues such as abortion or gay church leaders.

So, who "won"? A 2004 study showed that 26.3 % of the U.S. population considered themselves to be Evangelical Protestants – versus 16% that considered themselves part of mainline Protestantism.[52]

Evangelical Protestant	26.3
Mainline Protestant	16.0
Catholic	17.5

Certainly, much of the vitality in Protestantism seems to be on the Evangelical side, from Pentecostalism (rapidly growing in Africa), through megachurches in the United States, and through large-scale outreaches to youth, singles, and young couples with children.

At the end of the day, American Protestantism is indeed split into two camps – one that is focused on the saving grace of Christ, and one that is focused on a Social Gospel.

---

[52] *The American Religious Landscape and Political Attitudes: A Baseline for 2004* by John C. Green

Part Two – The Denominations

Part Two Introduction

As John Hagee has pointed out in the past, the age of the great Protestant denominations, which started in 1517 when Martin Luther tacked his 95 Theses on the door of Wittenburg Castle in Germany, is slowly coming to end. In the future, there will be really only two "sides" in Protestantism – those that believe that Jesus is the Son of God, and those that don't. However, at my various Bible studies, Sunday School classes, lectures and seminars, the most common question remains, "what is the difference between the denominations?" For historical purposes (if for no other), Part Two of this book will attempt to address that question.

Some caveats regarding Part Two of the book:

- By "denomination", I'm generally referring to a broad Protestant movement ("Presbyterian"), rather than a specific governmental body ("Presbyterian Church in America"), unless otherwise noted
- I generally only included denominations that have at least a million members in the United States. The only exception is the Anabaptists (Amish, Mennonites), who don't quite reach that mark. They are included because of their historical importance.
- I only included denominations that accept the basic Creeds of the Christian church (Apostles Creed, Nicene Creed, etc.)
- While I discuss the origins and early European histories of the various denominations, once the denominations were established in the United States, the focus becomes U.S.-centric in the time lines

Chapter Six - Anabaptists

Formed:	1525
Theology and practice:	Evangelical, pacifist, strict separation of church and state, marriage only among the "spiritually kindred", shunning/excommunication allowed in some circumstances, refusal to take oaths, foot washing, eschatological
Baptism:	Believer's
Sacraments:	Baptism and Communion
Form of government:	Decentralized (local bishops)
Worship:	Non-liturgical
Famous members:	Dwight Eisenhower (Mennonite roots), Milton Hershey, JM Smucker

The first Anabaptists were students of Ulrich Zwingli who became impatient with the slow pace of the Protestant Reformation. While much of the basic theology between Zwingli and the Anabaptists was similar, they disagreed on several key points, such as adult vs. infant baptism, separation of church and state, and whether Christians should serve in the military (the Anabaptists were nonviolent pacifists - Ulrich Zwingli died fighting the Catholics in the Second Battle of Kappel!)

Because of their break with Zwingli, and because their views were anathema to both Roman Catholics and other Protestant groups, the Anabaptists were the most persecuted group in the Reformation.

The first Mennonites came to the United States in 1683, and settled in Germantown, Pennsylvania. Because of Pennsylvania's (or William Penn's) reputation for religious tolerance, the Commonwealth became a target of Anabaptist migrations in the 17th and 18th century. Originally referred to as "Pennsylvania Deutsch", it was eventually corrupted into "Pennsylvania Dutch", which is how "outsiders" refer to them today.

Key events

Date	Event
c. 1525	Schism between Ulrich Zwingli and some of his students.
January 21, 1525	Anabaptist dissidents illegally rebaptize each other

Date	Event
1526	Zwingli authorizes execution of Anabaptists
1527	Schleitheim Confession of Faith
1534	Munster seized by Anabaptist revolutionaries
1536	Menno Simons joins Anabaptist movement
1632	Dordrecht Confession of Faith
1683	Mennonites settle in Germantown, Pennsylvania
1693	Schism over the doctrine of shunning results in formation of Amish
1748	*Martyrs Mirror* (1660) translated into German by Pennsylvania Mennonites
1750	A Mennonite schoolteacher, Christopher Dock, writes *Schul-Ordnung* (School Management) in Skippack, Pennsylvania
1860	General Conference Mennonite Church formed
1941 - 1945	40% of conscientious objectors in World War II were Amish or Mennonite
1965	Amish exempted from Social Security system
1972	Supreme Court Ruling in favor of Amish education practices - "There can be no assumption that today's majority is 'right' and the Amish and others are 'wrong'"
1979	Amish receive polio vaccinations
1987	PennDOT proposal to build a highway through the middle of Amish Country draws 1000 Amish to a public meeting
1988	Measles vaccinations
2000	319,768 Mennonites in North America[53]
2002	Mennonite Church U.S.A. formed
2003	1,203,995 members worldwide[54]

Key beliefs

The emergence of the Anabaptist movement rose out of their belief that there is no Biblical basis for infant baptism. Their mentor Ulrich Zwingli disagreed from both a theological point of view, and a secular one - infant baptism was used by the secular government for tax registration, and it was from the city government of Zurich that Zwingli had his authority.

In 1525, several of Zwingli's students (Conrad Grebel, Feliz Manz, Georg Blaurock) illegally rebaptized each other. The term "anabaptist" grew out of this event:

---

[53] http://www.mcusa-archives.org/Resources/membership.html
[54] http://www.mcusa-archives.org/Resources/membership.html

"The name Anabaptists which is now applied to them, has but lately come into use, deriving its matter from the matter of holy baptism, concerning which their views differ from those of all, so-called, Christendom."[55]

The Anabaptist view on infant baptism is summarized in the following passage:

"Of Holy Baptism, and why we have preferred it to all other articles, in our history: "...Because it is, beyond contradiction, the only article on account of which others call us Anabaptists. For, since all other so-called Christians have, yet without true foundation, this in common that they baptize infants; while with us the baptism only which is accompanied by faith and a penitent life, according to the word of God, is administered to adults..."[56]

The Anabaptists were also known (as the Amish are still known today) for their doctrine of "nonconformity", or the feeling that true Christians must separate themselves from the unclean world. The Anabaptists cite several scriptural references for this viewpoint, including Romans 12:2, 1 Peter 2:9-10, 2 Corinthians 6:14-18, 1 John 2:15-17, and Matthew 5:13-16.

Legacy

Compared to the other denominations discussed in this book, the Anabaptists are a small group today, with the Amish, Mennonites, and Hutterites comprising about 1,000,000 members worldwide (2003). However, while there is no unbroken line of succession between the Anabaptists and the modern day Baptists (over 32,000,000 strong in the U.S.A.), there is certainly great doctrinal similarity. The Anabaptists may be considered the spiritual predecessors of the American Baptist movement.

---

[55] *Martyrs Mirror* by Thielman J. van Braght, 1660
[56] *Ibid*

Amish farmer in Lancaster County, Pennsylvania (Photo by Robert Jones)

Chapter Seven - Anglican Church

Formed:	1534 (Act of Supremacy)
Theology and practice:	Evangelical, "great liberty in nonessentials", Book of Common Prayer, three pillars of Faith, Reason and Tradition, "sufficiency of scripture", "Catholicism with a small 'c'"
Baptism:	Adult and Children
Communion:	Communion as a spiritual mystery
Sacraments:	Baptism and Communion
Form of government:	Church of England is hierarchical - Archbishop of Canterbury, King or Queen Hierarchical; Episcopal Church is more decentralized, with congregations appointing their own priests
Worship:	Liturgical (very similar to Roman Catholic)
Famous members:	George Washington, Thomas Jefferson, James Madison, James Monroe, William Henry Harrison, John Tyler, Zachary Taylor, Franklin Pierce, Chester A. Arthur, Franklin Delano Roosevelt, Gerald Ford, George H. W. Bush, Leonidas Polk, Desmond TuTu

It can be said with some justification that the Reformation in England was based less on theological grounds, than on personal/political grounds (Henry VIII wanted a divorce). However, the English Reformation has had a profound and lasting effect on English speaking peoples everywhere, because of a) the establishment of the Church of England and b) William Tyndale's translation of the Bible, which served as the basis (90%) of the King James version of the Bible still in wide use today. Methodists, Baptsist and Congregationalists can all trace their origins to the Anglican Church.

Key Events

Date	Events
1408	The Church bans translation of the Bible into English (in response to Wycliffe and the Lollards)
c. 1493	Tyndale born in the west of England
1514/15	Tyndale receives M.A. at Oxford, ordained as priest
1520	Henry VIII publishes "Defense of the Seven Sacraments", refuting Luther - Named "Defender of the Faith" by the pope

Date	Events
1521	Tyndale acts as a tutor at a manor near Bath, and meets a woefully unlearned local clergy. Vows "If God spare my life, ere many years pass, I will cause a boy that driveth the plow shall know more of the Scriptures than thou dost."[57]
1524	Tyndale seeks permission of Bishop of London, Cuthbert Tunstall, to translate the Bible into English; refused
1524	Tyndale sails to Hamburg, Germany
1525	Tyndale completes translation of New Testament into English, from original Greek manuscripts. The print run in Cologne is interrupted by Catholic sympathizers.
1526	6,000 copies of Tyndale's English New Testament printed in Worms - many copies distributed in England
1527/29	Henry VIII seeks annulment from pope of his marriage; refused
1529/33	Battle of the pen between Tyndale and Sir Thomas More, Chancellor of England (More eventually wrote 9 books against the "Tyndale heresy"!)
1530	Tyndale's English translation of the first 5 books of the Old Testament printed in Antwerp
1534	Henry VIII leads passage of Act of Supremacy - Church of England is formed with King as head
1535	Tyndale betrayed by English spy Henry Phillips - imprisoned near Brussels
1535	Sir Thomas More ("A Man for All Seasons") beheaded for not publicly approving of marriage of Henry VIII to second wife (Ann Boleyn)
1535	First complete printed English translation of Bible published in England by Miles Coverdale - based largely on Tyndale's work
October 6, 1536	Tyndale burned at stake, in Brussels - Final words were, "Lord, open the king of England's eyes."
1536/40	Henry VIII and Thomas Cromwell systematically dissolve and destroy the monasteries in England
1549	Thomas Cranmer writes the first *Book of Common Prayer*
1553-1558	Queen Mary I restores Catholicism; 300 Protestant dissenters executed
1558 – 1603	Queen Elizabeth I restores the Church of England as the official religion of England; assumes title of Supreme Governor of the Church of England
1563	Convocation of the Church establishes the *Thirty-Nine Articles* as the doctrinal basis for the Anglican Church
1579	Sir Francis Drake's crew conducts first Anglican service in

---

[57] *Christian History*, Issue 16, 1987

Date	Events
	the New World
1607 - 1611	King James I appoints 54 men to make a new Bible translation, eventually called the King James Version
1607	First congregation at Jamestown
1689	King's Chapel in Boston opens
1693	William and Mary College established
1698	Churches established in Rhode Island and New York City
1775 - 1783	Disarray in the American version of the Church of England, as the Revolutionary War exposes divided loyalties
1782	*The Case of the Episcopal Churches in the United States Considered* published by William White – a call for unity
1783	Conference of churches in Maryland adopts the name Protestant Episcopal Church
1784	American Samuel Seabury ordained bishop in Scotland after cooling his heels for a year in England
1787	Archbishop of Canterbury ordains two new bishops from the United States
1789	First meeting of the House of Bishops – church constitution adopted in Philadelphia. Formal separation from the Church of England
1861 – 1864	Protestant Episcopal Church stays intact during the Civil War
1864	Bishop Leonidas Polk, Lt. General, C.S.A. killed at Battle of Pine Mountain, June 14, 1864
1881	English Revised Version of the New Testament published; 3,000,000 sold in first year
1888	Chicago Lambeth Quadrilateral on Church Unity
1970	Ordination of women as deacons approved
1976	Ordination of women as priests approved
1976 - 1979	Book of Common Prayer revised using contemporary language
1988	Barbara C. Harris elected first female bishop
1994	Episcopal Church - 2,471,880 members[58]
2006	House of Bishops endorses a resolution apologizing for its complicity in the institution of slavery

William Tyndale - key beliefs

While politically, Henry VIII was the founder of the Anglican Church, William Tyndale was its greatest early theologian. Tyndale was greatly influenced by John Wycliffe, Erasmus, and Martin Luther. He had a strong view that the

---

[58] *Handbook of Denominations in the United States*, by Frank S. Mead and Samuel S. Hill (Abingdon, 1995)

Bible should be both available and readable by the common man. He felt that true authority for faith is found only in the Bible.

One area where he disagreed with Martin Luther was on the subject of divorce. Tyndale felt that divorce is against God's will. It was this strong stand which eventually led to his death, as he rejected Henry VIII's entreaties to have Tyndale publicly back his divorce.

Tyndale's view on communion was Zwinglian - he stressed that communion was in commemoration of Christ's death.

Legacy of the English Reformation

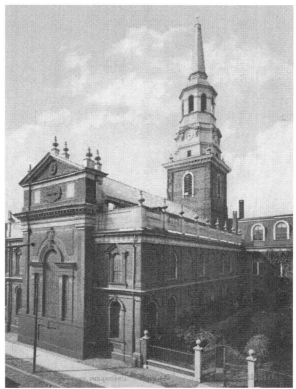

Christ Church in Philadelphia, worship home of George Washington [59]

Tyndale's translation of the Bible would form the basis of almost all other English translations for the next 400 years. His translation brought new words to the English language (longsuffering, peacemaker, scapegoat, beautiful), and used words and phrases that tended to undermine the traditional

[59] Library of Congress LC-DIG-ppmsca-18123

authority of the Roman Catholic Church, such as "congregation" instead of "church", "elders" instead of "priests", and "repentance" instead of "penance". 90% of Tyndale's words appeared in the King James Version of Bible, and 75% of Tyndale's words appeared in the Revised Standard Version of Bible.[60]

The English Reformation produced the Church of England, headed by the sovereign, and the Episcopal Church in the United States, which has approximately 2,500,000 members.

---

[60] *Christian History*, Issue 16

Chapter Eight - Baptists

Formed:	1609
Theology and practice:	Evangelical, evangelistic, typically Calvinist, eschatological (usually premillenialist)
Baptism:	Believer's, immersion
Sacraments:	Baptism and Communion
Form of government:	Decentralized
Worship:	Non-Liturgical
Famous members:	Warren G. Harding, Harry S. Truman, Jimmy Carter, William Jefferson Clinton, Hillary Clinton

> "The true constitution of the Church is of a new creature baptized into the Father, the Son, and the Holy Ghost: **The false constitution is of infants baptized**: we profess therefore that all those Churches that baptize infants are of the same false constitution: and all those Churches that baptize the new creature, those that are made Disciples by teaching, men confessing their faith and their sins, are of one true constitution..."
> – John Smyth, "The Character of the Beast", 1609[61]

The Baptist movement grew out of the Puritan/Separatist movements in England in the 17th century. The Puritans, generally Calvinists, wanted the Church of England to be more democratic in its governmental structure, and less Catholic in its trappings, liturgy, and rituals. (The Puritans were members of the Church of England, who wished to "purify" the church from within.) The Separatists were more radical, desiring a complete break from the Church of England. Out of the Separatist movement came both the Pilgrims and the Baptists.

The man often cited as the "first" Baptist is John Smyth (1570–1612), a former Anglican priest that became, in succession, a Puritan, a Separatist, and finally, a Baptist. In 1608, John Smyth (with the help of Thomas Helwys (?–1616)) took a group of Separatist followers to Amsterdam. During this period, Mennonites, descendants of the 16th century Anabaptists influenced Smyth and his followers.

In 1609, in a scene somewhat reminiscent of the Anabaptist "re-baptizing" ceremony in Zurich 90 years before, Smyth re-baptized himself and 40 fol-

---

[61] *The Baptists: A People Who Gathered "To Walk in All His Ways."*: Christian History, Issue 6

lowers, reasoning that their baptisms as infants were invalid. What was soon to become the Baptist Church had begun.

In 1644, a group of Calvinist Particular Baptists published their "London Confession", affirming believers' baptism as a key tenet:

> **"Baptism is an ordinance of the New Testament, given by Christ, to be dispersed only upon persons professing faith.** The way and manner of dispensing this Ordinance the Scripture holds to be **dipping or plunging the whole body under water**." - "The London Confession (1644)"[62]

There are approximately 32 million Baptists in the United States today

Key Events

Date	Events
1608	John Smyth takes a group of Separatist followers to Amsterdam, and is greatly influenced by Mennonites he finds there
1609	Smyth re-baptizes himself and 40 followers
1612	Death of John Smyth
1638	Calvinist Particular Baptist Church founded in England
1639	Separatist minister Roger Williams establishes a Baptist church in Providence, Rhode Island
1641	John Clarke establishes a Baptist church in Newport, RI
1644	Calvinist Particular Baptists publish their "London Confession", affirming believer's baptism as a key tenet
1689	Philadelphia Confession written by Baptist Churches in London
18th century	• George Whitfield preaches doctrine of free will in the Americas • Split among Baptists into "Old Lights" (rationalists) and "New Lights" (more focused on the impact of the Holy Spirit and emotionalism) • Black Baptist churches begin to be formed in the South
1793	73,471 Baptists in the U.S., 25% of them Black[63]
1814	General Missionary Convention of the Baptist Denomination in the United States of America for Foreign Missions
1832	New Hampshire State Baptist Convention writes a confes-

---

[62] The Baptists: A People Who Gathered "To Walk in All His Ways." Christian History, Issue 6, 1985

[63] *Handbook of Denominations in the United States*, by Frank S. Mead and Samuel S. Hill (Abingdon, 1995)

Date	Events
	sion
1836	Providence Baptist Association of Ohio – first organized Black group
1845	Southern Baptist Convention formed
1895	National Baptist Convention of Americas formed, consolidating various Black Baptist groups
1905	Baptist World Alliance formed
1961	Progressive National Baptist Convention of Americas formed
1994	32 million Baptists in 27 denominations in the U.S.[64]
2000	Southern Baptist Convention upholds its long-standing prohibition on female pastors
2005	Lynn Swanson Fowler ordained as a Music Minister at First Baptist Church in Marietta, GA

Baptism by immersion[65]

[64] *Ibid*
[65] Library of Congress LC-USZC4-3265

Chapter Nine - Lutherans

Formed:	1517 (Luther and the 95 Theses) or 1530 (Augsburg Confession)
Theology and practice:	Evangelical (Luther wrote the book); *Sola scriptura, Sola Gratia, Sola Fide*, priesthood of believers
Baptism:	Adult and Children
Communion:	Body and blood of Christ are present "in, with, and under the forms" of bread and wine during communion
Sacraments:	Baptism and Communion
Form of government:	Centralized (local congregations vote for pastors)
Worship:	Liturgical
Famous members[66]:	Bach, Beethoven, Mendelssohn, Steve Jobs, Henry Melchoir Muhlenberg, Norman Schwarzkopf, Richard John Neuhaus, Edwin Meese III, William Rehnquist, Dag Hammarskold, Dr. Albert Schweitzer

While other groups that eventually became Protestants preceded Luther (Moravians, Waldensians), the Protestant Reformation as we know it today can reasonably be traced to the actions of an obscure Augustinian Monk named Martin Luther, who, in two acts of defiance, changed the face of Europe forever, both secularly, and in terms of Christianity. The two acts - tacking his 95 theses to door of Wittenburg Castle in 1517, and his "Here I stand, I can do no other" response to the Emperor of the Holy Roman Empire in 1521.

---

[66] http://www.faithlutherangroton.org/famous.html

Dr. Martin Luther[67]

Key Events

Date	Events
1483	Martin Luther born in Eisleben, Saxony
1505/07	Becomes Augustinian monk; ordained as a priest
1512	Doctorate in Theology; Professor of Biblical Literature at Wittenburg University
1517	Protests sale of indulgences by Pope Leo X
October 31, 1517	Tacks 95 theses to door of Wittenburg Castle
1520	Bull of Excommunication #1
Dec, 10/11, 1520	Luther burns the Bull; announces that to be saved, one must renounce the Pope
1521	Bull of Excommunication #2 - Luther excommunicated
April 17/18, 1521	Council (Diet) of Worm, convened by Charles V, Emperor of the Holy Roman Empire. Luther ordered to recant. Luther replied, "Here I stand. I can do no other."

[67] Library of Congress LC-DIG-pga-02205

Date	Events
1521-1522	Luther in hiding at Wartburg Castle; translates New Testament into German, and battles with the Devil
March 9, 1522	Luther begins a series of sermons asking for calm as followers of Carlstadt destroy relics, paintings and statuary in churches
1525	Marries former nun Katherine von Bora; criticizes the Peasant's Revolt
1527	Writes "A Mighty Fortress is Our God" (Luther wrote a total of 41 hymns)
1528	Publishes "Large Catechism", "Small Catechism"
1530	Luther is the doctrinal inspiration for the Augsburg Confession, written by Philip Melancthon
1534	Publishes German Bible - 100,000 copies of New Testament printed in Wittenberg during his lifetime[68]
1546	Death of Luther
1577	Formula of Concord
1619	Lutheran service at Hudson Bay
1623	Lutheran congregation in Manhattan
1738	Lutherans in Georgia open first orphanage in America
1748	Henry Melchior Muhlenberg establishes first Lutheran synod in America – the Ministerium of Pennsylvania
1820	First General Synod
1826	The Lutheran Theological Seminary at Gettysburg, Pennsylvania, is established
1840 - 1873	58 Lutheran synods formed in the U.S.[69]
1847	Missouri Synod formed
1850	The first deaconess is consecrated in North America
1863	United Synod of the South created
1866	Several other synods (including Pennsylvania) pull out of the General Synod, and form the General Council
1917	Norwegian Lutheran Church of America formed, uniting three Lutheran groups
1918	Joint Synod of Wisconsin formed
1918	North and South reunite in United Lutheran Church, as well as reunification of the General Synod and the General Council
1930	American Lutheran Church merges synods of Iowa, Ohio and Buffalo

---

[68] *The Reformation* by Will Durant (MJF Books, 1957)
[69] http://www.elca.org/communication/quick.html

Date	Events
1970	Elizabeth Platz becomes the first female Lutheran pastor in North America
1988	Evangelical Lutheran Church in America formed; 5.2 million members in 1994[70]
1992	April Ulring Larson becomes first woman bishop in America
1999	Arts & Entertainment network votes Luther the 3rd most influential person of the millennium
October 31, 1999	"The Joint Declaration on the Doctrine of Justification" is signed by the Catholic Church and the Lutheran Church, seemingly bringing the Catholic Church closer to Luther's view of salvation by "faith alone"
2006	Evangelical Lutheran Church has 4,930,429 members[71]
2006	Missouri Synod has 2,463,747 members[72]

Key Beliefs

Luther had struggled his whole clerical life with the idea that God was a wrathful, judgmental God, and that no mortal man could possibly live a life pure enough to please God. One day, while sitting on the privy in Wittenburg Castle, Luther had what he later described as a "thunderbolt to my conscience" - the realization that the righteousness of God is not a negative characteristic (i.e. judgmental), but rather a merciful one (justification of sinners through faith). Romans 1:17 was the spark for this revelation:

> "For therein is the righteousness of God revealed from faith to faith: as it is written, The just shall live by faith."" (KJV)

Later, Romans 1:17 would become the centerpiece of Luther's theology, capsulizing his views on justification by faith, and salvation by grace, and grace alone:

> "The righteousness of God is the cause of our salvation. This righteousness, however, is not that according to which God Himself is righteous as God, but that by which we are justified by Him through faith in the Gospel. It is called the righteousness of God in contradistinction to man's righteousness which comes from works...righteousness (justification) precedes works and good works grow out of it."[73]

---

[70] *Handbook of Denominations in the United States*
[71] http://www.elca.org/communication/quick.html
[72] http://www.lcms.org/pages/internal.asp?NavID=2436
[73] Luther's Commentary on Romans

Luther was also a strong proponent of viewing the Bible as the sole source of Christian belief. He vociferously rejected non-Biblical tenets such as purgatory, worship of Mary and the Saints, and indulgences (although not infant baptism). He generally viewed the Bible as literally true (what would be called fundamentalism today), but at the same time, he cast some doubt on the authority of several books in the Bible, including James, Hebrews, and Revelation.

Luther strongly rejected monasticism, which he viewed as the epitome of the "salvation through works" viewpoint. (The Augsburg Confession had numerous references rejecting monasticism.) He also rejected clerical celibacy, and he eventually married a former nun, and had 6 children! However, because he only accepted two of seven Roman sacraments - Baptism and Communion, he viewed that divorce was possible, since he did not accept marriage as a sacrament.

Luther also strongly believed in the Pauline/Augustinian doctrine of predestination, although the doctrine is surprisingly under-represented in the Augsburg Confession, upon which the Lutheran faith is based.

Luther was also a strong proponent of the doctrine of a "priesthood of believers", a view which says that each Christian can make their own interpretation of the Scriptures, and that no intermediaries (such as clerics) are needed for a Christian to communicate with God. Coming out of this viewpoint was Luther's total rejection of papal authority. He noted that, in the first several centuries of the Church, the Bishop of Rome had no special authority.

One area where Luther's views strongly disagreed with that of other Reformers (Zwingli, Schwenckfeld, the Anabaptists) was in the area of the nature of the Eucharist (Communion). While Luther rejected the Roman Catholic doctrine of Transubstantiation (defined by the Fourth Lateran Council in 1215) which said that the elements actually turned into the body and blood of Christ during the Eucharist, Luther's Consubstantiation view still promulgated the presence of Christ's body and blood during communion:

> "It is the true body and blood of our Lord Jesus Christ, under the bread and wine, given unto us Christians to eat and to drink, as it was instituted by Christ himself."[74]

---

[74] Luther's "Small Catechism", Schaff, Vol. III, p. 90

In 1530, the Lutheran Church as we know it today was created with the signing of the Augsburg Confession, written by Philip Melancthon (and inspired by Luther).

Legacy

So why did the theological views of an obscure Augustinian monk light the match that ignited the Protestant Reformation, when earlier reformers such as Wycliffe and Hus had much less impact? If one were to pick a single factor, it would have to be the development of the printing press. As the Internet today has democratized the distribution of information and opinion, the printing press allowed views at odds with official Catholicism to receive wide-spread (and International) exposure.   Europe in the 16th century was ready for a message of reform, and Luther and the printing press delivered it.

It is hard to put into words the effect of Martin Luther. By successfully refuting the pope and his bull of excommunication, Luther lessened the hegemony of the Roman Church over Europe. By successfully refuting the Emperor of the Holy Roman Empire, Luther helped bring about the rise of nationalism. And, of course, Luther was the spark that ignited the Reformation, which forever changed the face of Christianity in the world.

Luther's influence continues in modern times. On October 31, 1999 in Augsburg, a *Joint Declaration on the Doctrine of Justification* was signed by the Lutheran World Federation and the Catholic Church. Among the contents:

> "Together we confess: By grace alone, in faith in Christ's saving work and not because of any merit on our part, we are accepted by God and receive the Holy Spirit, who renews our hearts while equipping and calling us to good works."[75]

This understanding of justification by faith would seemingly bring the Catholic Church closer to Luther's interpretation.

Other legacies of Luther include:

---

[75] http://www.lutheranworld.org/Special_Events/EN/jd97e.pdf

- As the founder of the Lutheran Church, Martin Luther could view with satisfaction that there are over 65,000,000 Lutherans world-wide as of 2002[76]
- Luther was the first to use the term "evangelical" to describe the essential Reformation theology. By some estimates, there are over 65 million evangelical Christians in the United States today.
- Luther was the first proponent of congregational hymn singing in church
- Luther wrote what many consider to be the greatest hymn of all time – *A Mighty Fortress is Our God*

---

[76] http://www.wfn.org/2002/08/msg00041.html

Chapter Ten - Methodists

Formed:	1729 (Holy Club) or 1739 (Methodist Societ-ies)
Theology and practice:	Evangelical, Free Will, Prevenient Grace, Spir-it-focused (at least in the early days), wide freedom of personal belief and interpretation
Baptism:	Adults, Children
Sacraments:	Baptism and Communion
Form of government:	Centralized (Bishops appoint pastors)
Worship:	Non-Liturgical
Famous members[77]:	George Whitefield, William McKinley, George W. Bush, James Knox Polk, Ulysses S Grant, Rutherford B. Hayes, Rush Limbaugh, George McGovern, Harry Blackmun, Ralph Reed, Wil-liam Foxwell Albright, Zell Miller, Richard B. Russell, Johnny Isakson, Roy Barnes

John Wesley preaching[78]

John Wesley was born in 1703, the son of an Anglican rector. Along with his brother Charles (b. 1707), they formed the "Holy Club" at Oxford in 1729. The Holy Club was half Bible study, and half monastic lay order. Among the

---

[77] http://www.adherents.com/largecom/fam_meth.html
[78] Library of Congress LC-USZC2-2716

facets of the Holy Club was the study of scriptures, following a strict moral code, periodic fasting, and a focus on a prison ministry.

The Holy Club was formed in response to the lax nature of the observing of religion (Church of England) at Oxford in those days. Charles Wesley later commented on the origin of the name "Methodist":

> "I went to the weekly sacrament and persuaded two or three young students to accompany me to observe the method of study prescribed by the University, that gained me the harmless name of Methodist."[79]

Although both were long ordained in the Anglican Church, John and Charles would both have "born again" experiences in 1538, beginning a sequence of events that would lead to the creation of the Methodist Church.

John's conversion experience would occur on May 24, 1738 at Aldersgate, when he was listening to a Moravian speaker reading from the preface to Luther's Commentary on Romans:

> "In the evening, I went very unwillingly to a Society in Aldersgate-Street, where one was reading Luther's preface to the Epistle to the Romans. About a quarter before nine, while he was describing the change which God works in the heart through faith in Christ, I felt my heart strangely warmed. I felt I did trust in Christ; Christ alone, for salvation; and an assurance was given me, that he had taken away my sins, even mine, and saved me from the law of sin and death."[80]

Charles' conversion happened several days earlier. On May 17, 1738, Charles was greatly influenced by reading Luther's Commentary on Galatians. On May 21, 1738, he heard the words "In the name of Jesus of Nazareth, arise, and believe, and thou shalt be healed of all thy infirmities", spoken by the sister of the man with whom he was rooming. Charles would later comment, "I now found myself at peace with God, and rejoice in hope of loving Christ."

For the next several decades, both Charles and John preached temperance, hard work, salvation and faith in Christ to workers and prisoners all over the British Isles, on horseback and on foot. By one estimate, John rode over

---

[79] Charles Wesley, on the Holy Club
[80] John Wesley's Journal, May 24, 1738

250,000 miles on horseback and preached over 40,000 sermons! He traveled 42 times to Ireland and 22 times to Scotland. [81]

While the first "Methodist Societies" were established in 1739, John Wesley didn't break from the Anglican Church until 1784. As an Anglican priest, he was not able to ordain Methodist ministers in the United States, so he left the Church of England.

Date	Events
1728	John Wesley ordained as a priest at Oxford
1729	Charles Wesley founds the Holy Club at Oxford
1735	Charles Wesley ordained, Church of England
1735/37	Wesleys mission to Georgia
1738	John and Charles Wesley have separate conversion experiences within several days of each other
1739	First "Methodist Societies" formed
1739 – 1743	Charles preaches to over 150,000 people
1766	First Methodist Societies in the U.S.
1769	Methodists in New York build the Wesley Chapel
1769-1771	John Wesley sends lay ministers to the Colonies, including Francis Asbury
1773	First Methodist Conference held, in Philadelphia
1776-1779	Many Methodist preachers and congregants, loyal to England, flee to Canada or England
1784	John Wesley breaks with the Anglican Church (Deed of Declaration)
1784	Christmas Conference in Baltimore organizes Methodist Episcopal Church and appoints first bishops
1785	The Methodist Episcopal Church publishes its first *Book of Discipline*
1789	The Methodists establish the first church book publishing house in America
1792	First General Conference held
1816	The African Methodist Episcopal Church formed
1844	General Conference asks a Southern Bishop to stop practicing his office as long as he remains a slaveholder
1845	Split of Methodists into Methodist Episcopal Church, Northern Body and Methodist Episcopal Church, South
1908	The Methodist Episcopal Church adopts a Social Creed at its General Conference
1913	4,000,000 Methodists[82]

---

[81] *Christian History*, Issue 69, 2001
[82] http://archives.umc.org/interior.asp?mid=1215

Date	Events
Post World War I	Methodist church strongly supports temperance movement
1938	Methodist Episcopal Church, Northern Body and Methodist Episcopal Church, South reunite
1939	7.7 million members after unification[83]
1956	Women accepted into the clergy
April 23, 1968	The United Methodist Church was created, bringing together The Evangelical United Brethren Church and The Methodist Church. The new UMC had 11,000,000 members[84]
1980	Marjorie Matthews becomes first female bishop
1994	13 million Methodists in the U.S.; 18 million around the world[85]
2003	"The United Methodist Church has about 8.3 million members in the United States and 1.5 million members in Europe, Africa and the Philippines."[86]

Key Beliefs

The Wesleys were influenced by several sources, including (obviously), the Anglican Church in which they were both ordained priests. John thought the Church of England was focused too much on rationality, not enough on the spirit. This Wesleyan focus on the Holy Spirit would later blossom in the 18th and 19th century religious revivals in the United States.

John Wesley was also greatly influenced by Martin Luther and John Calvin, although he broke with them on one key issue - predestination. John Wesley was an Arminian, believing strongly in the doctrine of Free Will, and also in the doctrine of Prevenient Grace, which states:

> "...the divine love that surrounds all humanity and precedes any and all of our conscious impulses. This grace prompts our first wish to please God, our first glimmer of understanding concerning God's will, and our 'first slight transient conviction' of having sinned against God. God's grace also awakens in us an earnest longing for deliverance from sin and death and moves us toward repentance and faith." [87]

---

[83] *Ibid*

[84] *Ibid*

[85] *Ibid*

[86] *Membership*, 5/3/2003, United Methodist Church Archives

[87] *The Book of Discipline of The United Methodist Church - 2004* (United Methodist Publishing House, 2004)

John Wesley was also greatly influenced by the Moravians (descendants of followers of John Hus), whom he originally met on the ship back from Georgia in 1737.

Legacy

"American Methodists proceeding to their camp meeting"[88]

The Methodist Church in the United States was a great influence on the *Great Awakening* in the United States in the 18th century, as well as subsequent religious revivals in the 19th century. Methodists would greatly influence the Holiness movement of the mid-19th century, as well as the Pentecostal movement that arose in the late-19th century.

Charles Wesley wrote between 6,500-9,000 hymns, many of them still sung today in Protestant (and even Catholic) churches throughout the world. Some of Charles Wesley's greatest works include:

- "O for a Thousand Tongues to Sing"
- "Hark, the Herald Angels Sing"
- "And Can It Be?"
- "Come, Thou Long-Expected Jesus"
- "Love Divine, All Loves Excelling"

---

[88] Library of Congress LC-USZC4-3264

- "Christ the Lord is Risen today"

Today in the United States, the United Methodist Church is the third largest Christian denomination (after the Roman Catholic Church and the Southern Baptist Convention).

Chapter Eleven - Pentecostal Movement

Aimee Semple McPherson[89]

Formed:	c. 1900
Theology and practice:	Evangelical, Spirit-filled, charismatic, fundamentalist, often Free Will, divine healing, speaking in tongues as a sign of baptism by the Holy Spirit, eschatological. Early in the movement, many were pacifistic. (Note: only a very tiny portion of Pentecostals are involved in snake handling)
Baptism:	Believer's, immersion. Baptism by the Holy Spirit. Will sometimes do rebaptisms for backsliders.
Sacraments:	Baptism and Communion

---

[89] Library of Congress LC-F8- 40994[P&P]

Form of government:	(Very) decentralized
Worship:	Non-Liturgical
Famous members[90]:	Oral Roberts, Jim Bakker, Jimmy Swaggart, John Ashcroft, James Watt, Elvis Presley, Denzel Washington, Anthony Quinn, Pat Boone, Aimee Semple McPherson, Al Sharpton

The Pentecostal movement is the largest Protestant denomination in the world today, by some accounts approaching 500,000,000 adherents[91]. (Note: not all Pentecostal churches have formal membership programs).

The Pentecostal movement had its beginnings in the Holiness movement of the mid-19th century. The Holiness movement itself grew out of the Spirit-filled Methodist tradition, and resulted in a second wave (the first wave occurred in the 18th century) of revival meetings sweeping throughout the United States.

In the late 19th century, a Kansas college student named Charles Fox Parham promulgated a theory of *glossolalia* – speaking in tongues – as evidence of baptism of the Holy Spirit. In time, his theory would spread like wildfire across the Midwest, and make its way all the way to Los Angeles.

In 1903, a southern Holiness preacher named William J. Seymour opened the Azusa Street Revival. His first sermon was on the Pentecost (Acts 2:4), and the modern Pentecostal movement was born.

Pentecostalism reached a mass audience in the 1910s and 1920s when Aimee Semple McPherson became a national sensation as a Pentecostal revivalist. She drove around in a "gospel car", with signs on it such as "Where will you spend eternity?"

Key Events

Date	Event
1867	National Holiness Camp Meeting Association formed
1896	Speaking in tongues occurs at a Holiness meeting in North Carolina
1900	Charles Fox Parham opens a Bible school in Topeka, Kansas
1901	Speaking in tongues occurs at a Holiness meeting in

[90] http://www.adherents.com/adh_fam.html
[91] *Christian History*, Issue 58, 1998

Date	Event
	Topeka, Kansas
1903	A revival in Galena, Kansas gains thousands of converts to Charles Parham's message
1905	*The Great Revival in Wales* published, introducing a larger audience to what would become Pentecostalism
1906	The Azusa Street Revival in Los Angeles, led by William J. Seymour becomes the foundation of the modern Pentecostal movement
1906	First General Assembly of the Church of God, in Cleveland Tennessee
1907	Pentecostal Assemblies of the World organized
1910	Tennessee preacher George W. Hensley handles a rattlesnake in front of his congregation
1913	Pentecostal-Holiness meeting held in Arroyo Seco, California, attended primarily by Pentecostal pastors
1914	First General Counsel of the Assemblies of God; receives ordained women into fellowship
1919	Aimee Semple McPherson becomes a national sensation as a Pentecostal revivalist. She drove around in a "gospel car", with signs on it such as "Where will you spend eternity?"
1922	Death of William J. Seymour
1926	Aimee Semple McPherson somewhat discredited in what may have been a phony kidnapping
1943	Pentecostal churches join the National Association of Evangelicals
1998	Largest church in the world is the Yoido Full Gospel Church in Korea – 240,000 attend weekly worship[92]
2006	Assemblies of God has 12,100 churches in the U.S.; 236,022 churches and outstations in 191 other nations[93]

---

[92] *Christian History*, Issue 58, 1998
[93] http://ag.org/top/about/history.cfm

Chapter Twelve - Presbyterian Church

Formed:	1525 (Zwingli); 1560 (Scottish Presbyterian Church)
Theology and practice:	Evangelical, Calvinist, predestination, Bible is inspired by God, but written by man, rationalistic
Baptism:	Adults, Children
Communion:	Symbolic
Sacraments:	Baptism and Communion
Form of government:	Decentralized ("Presbyterian")
Worship:	Non-Liturgical
Famous members[94]:	John Witherspoon, Andrew Jackson, James Buchanan, Grover Cleveland, Benjamin Harrison, Woodrow Wilson, Condoleezza Rice, Aaron Burr, Dan Quayle, Bob Dole/Elizabeth Dole, Warren Burger, William O. Douglas, William Jennings Bryan, Billy Sunday, Andrew Carnegie, Ross Perot, Sam Walton, J. Edgar Hoover, Alger Hiss, Roy Rogers

Presbyterianism was founded by three Protestant Reformers in the 16th century. One was Swiss (Ulrich Zwingli), one was French (John Calvin), and one was Scottish (John Knox).

Ulrich Zwingli (1484-1531)

Key Events

Date	Events
1484	Ulrich Zwingli born in Wildhaus, Switzerland
1506	Master of Arts, University of Basel; becomes a priest - Influenced by writings of Erasmus
1518	Appointed preacher at Grossmunster Cathedral in Zurich - Leads Zurich to withdrawal from alliance with Catholic France
1522	Resigns from priesthood; employed by Zurich City Council as evangelical pastor
1523	Publishes 67 theses
1525/1526	Authorizes execution of the Anabaptists
1531	Dies fighting in Catholic/Protestant Second War of Kappel

---

[94] http://www.adherents.com/largecom/fam_pres.html

Key beliefs

Zwingli, a contemporary, not a follower of Luther, laid the foundation for the Reformed Church. As Luther, he believed that mankind is unregenerate, and is saved through the intercession of Christ. Also as Luther, he believed in the supreme authority of the Bible.

Zwingli also believed in predestination, and took it to some interesting conclusions. He felt that it would be impossible for God to be omnipotent and omnipresent if he did not "control and dispose" all events. As Zwingli believed that we were predestined to salvation (or damnation) before birth, this meant that there may be members of the elect among the heathen (Luther was horrified), and that infants that died before being baptized may be saved, if they were predestined to be so.

Zwingli believed that baptism by water can take place without baptism of the Holy Spirit, and that baptism by the Holy Spirit can take place without baptism by water. In the latter case, the believer is still saved. Zwingli also believed in infant baptism, a point in which he violently disagreed with his students, the Anabaptists. To Zwingli, an important element of infant baptism is a profession of faith by the parents, and a pledge to bring the child up as a Christian.

It was the doctrine of what happens during the Eucharist (communion) that caused the biggest rift between Luther and Zwingli. Unlike Luther, who believed that Christ's body and blood were present during the sacrament, Zwingli took a more symbolic view. He felt that the bread and wine signify the body and blood of Christ - he therefore rejected transubstantiation and consubstantiation. He further believed that the sacrament was a commemoration, not a repetition (as in the Catholic faith) of the atoning sacrifice of Christ. To Zwingli, communion is a visible sign of an invisible grace.

Legacy

Generally, most Church historians view that two primary movements came out of the Protestant Reformation - Lutheran, and the Reformed Faith. Zwingli was the founder of the Reformed faith, which begat groups such as the Presbyterians (Knox), Puritans, the Reformed Church in Europe, the Anabaptists etc.

Zwingli also initiated the practice of sermon-centric church services.

Statue to Zwingli in Zurich (Photo by Barbara Brim)

John Calvin (1509-1564)

John Calvin[95]

Key Events

Date	Events
1509	John Calvin born in Noyon, France
1523	Studies for priesthood in Paris
1528/29	Studies law in Orleans, Bourges
1533	"Conversion" - Breaks with Roman Church; flees to Geneva Switzerland (1536)
1536	• Publishes "Institutes of the Christian Religion" • Flees to Geneva Switzerland, which declared for the Reformed Faith two months before Calvin arrived • At the urging of William Farel, becomes an evangelical preacher in Geneva
April 23,	Farel and Calvin deposed by the Great Council of Geneva – Calv-

[95] Library of Congress LC-USZ62-72002

Date	Events
1538	in goes to Strasbourg, Farel to Basel
1540	Calvin marries Idelette de Bure
1541	Prodded by commercial interests, and fear of a revived Catholicism, the Great Council asked Farel and Calvin to return to Geneva
1541/1564	Theocratic ruler of the "City of God" in Geneva, Switzerland
1542	"Ecclesiastical Ordinances" passed - Government of the Reformed Church established (no bishops, cardinals, etc.)
1610	Long after Calvin's death, Dutch Calvinist's debate Arminians (believers in free will) in Dort; the Calvinist's develop the acronym TULIP to describe Calvin's theology.

Key beliefs

John Calvin's theology, fairly or unfairly, will forever be associated with the acronym TULIP, which was actually defined by 17th-century Dutch Calvinists in their debate with the free will Arminians in 1610.

Although Calvin never used the acronym himself, it is at least useful to illustrate some of Calvin's basic theological tenets:

- **Total Depravity** - Calvin, like Luther, felt that NO ONE was worthy of salvation (see Romans 3:9-18), and that there was NOTHING that man could do to save himself.
  Unconditional Election - Calvin was a strong proponent of the doctrine of predestination. In fact, Calvin went so far as to define a doctrine of "double election" meaning that everyone was predestined to either salvation or damnation before they were born. Thus, no works by man had any effect on God's election.
  Limited Atonement - This view stated that, while God's death on the cross was sufficient to save all of mankind, it was efficient only to save those that were predestined for salvation.
  Irresistible Grace - If one was predestined for salvation, it was impossible to reject God's grace (through free will).
  Perseverance of the Saints - Those that are truly predestined for salvation, and justified by their faith, will not reject salvation.

Calvin was also a strong believer in the concept of the Universal Church, which he defined as being the congregation of the elect, living, dead, or to be born.

Legacy

John Calvin was the preeminent theologian of his time, and perhaps one of the 2 or 3 greatest theologians in history. He continued Zwingli's Reformed Church, out of which the Presbyterian, European Reformed churches, French Huguenots, and English Puritans grew. He wrote the most complete theology of Protestantism ever written – *Christian Institutes*, which is still the foundation of much of Protestantism today. His views on God and work would later be known as the "Protestant Work Ethic", which was a key to the success of the industrial revolution in the United States in the 19th century.

Calvin's views on the desirability of democratically electing leaders would later be adopted by the Presbyterian Church, and still exists today. Calvinists in 18th century America would influence the American Revolution and the U.S. Constitution.

Calvin's view that unjust rulers or dictators could be removed by the populace was put into very practical use in World War II resistance movements, and in anti-Communist resistance movements in Eastern Europe after World War II.

John Knox (1514(?)-1572)

"The preaching of John Knox, before the Lords of the congregation in St. Andrews 1559"[96]

---

[96] Library of Congress LC-DIG-pga-01692

Key Events

Date	Events
1514(?)	John Knox born in Haddington, Scotland
c. 1532	Ordained priest
1546	Protestant preacher George Wishart executed as heretic (Knox was his bodyguard)
1547	Joins revolt against the Roman Church in Scotland; becomes preacher to the revolutionaries
1547	Captured during siege of castle of St. Andrews; made a galley slave
1549	Released from galley imprisonment - preaches in England; confessor to Edward VI
1554	Flees England of Catholic Mary Tudor to Geneva - Becomes student of John Calvin
1559	Returns to Scotland; preaches against idolatry - followers sack monasteries
1560	Scottish Parliament establishes Presbyterian Church of Scotland
1560/67	Fights to depose Catholic Mary, Queen of Scots (deposed 1567)
1587	Mary, Queen of Scots beheaded by Elizabeth I

John Knox had perhaps the most colorful life of all of the 16th century reformers. Among his varied roles:

- Bodyguard to an Evangelical preacher
- Galley slave under the French
- Personal confessor to King Edward VI of England
- Preacher in Calvin's Geneva to English-speaking residents
- Father of the Presbyterian Church of Scotland
- Key figure in the overthrow of Mary, Queen of Scots

Legacy

While Presbyterians often trace their theological roots to Ulrich Zwingli and John Calvin, John Knox can quite legitimately be referred to as "the father of Presbyterianism". In the United States, Presbyterians number approximately 3,000,000 members.

Presbyterians in America

Key Events

Date	Event
1611	First Presbyterian congregation in America, in Virginia

Date	Event
1630	Congregations in New England
1643	Congregation in New York
1643-1648	Westminster Assembly of Divines produces Larger and Shorter Catechisms, and the Westminster Confession (1648)
1683	Francis Makemie organizes five churches in Maryland
1706	First American Presbytery at Philadelphia
1716	First synod, comprised of four presbyteries
1726	Rev. William Tennent founds a ministerial 'log college' in Pennsylvania
1729	General Synod accepts the Westminster Confession, and the Shorter and Longer Catechisms
1740	Presbyterian Church splits over feud between "new side" revivalists and "old side" Calvinists
1757	Reunification from the 1740 split
1776	Rev. John Witherspoon, a Presbyterian minister, signs the Declaration of Independence
1776-1783	30 Presbyterian ministers enroll in Continental Army as chaplains
1789	First General Assembly
1812 - 1836	Theological seminaries created, including Princeton and Columbia
1837	More splits in the church - "Old School" vs. "New School" – over missionary expenditures, and over partnership with the Congregationalists
1846	"New School" Presbyterians condemn slavery
1861	47 "Old School" presbyteries form the Presbyterian Church in the Confederate States of America
1867	Southern churches form the Presbyterian Church in the United States (PCUS)
1870	"Old School" and "New School" churches reunite in the North
1931	Women admitted to role of Ruling Elder
1957	Women admitted to the clergy – none were actually ordained until 1965
1958	Merger of Northern churches forms United Presbyterian Church in the U.S.A.
1967	Confession of 1967 passed in the UPCUSA
June 10, 1983	United Presbyterian Church in the U.S.A. and the Presbyterian Church in the United States reunite (North and South). 3,1666,050 members[97]

---

[97] *Handbook of Denominations in the United States*, by Frank S. Mead and Samuel S. Hill (Abingdon, 1995)

Date	Event
2006	"The church [PCUSA] has a membership of 2,405,311 in all fifty states and Puerto Rico. Presently there are 11,064 congregations, 21,194 ordained ministers, 894 candidates for ministry, and 101,324 elders."[98]

[98] http://www.pcusa.org/101/101-whoare.htm

Chapter Thirteen - United Church of Christ

Formed:	1630 (in America)
Theology and practice:	Evangelical, Calvinist (including predestination); In more recent times, "progressive"
Baptism:	Adults, children
Communion:	Symbolic
Sacraments:	Baptism and communion
Form of government:	Decentralized (basic tenet of Congregationalism)
Worship:	Non-liturgical
Famous members:	Jonathan Edwards, Martin Van Buren (Dutch Reformed), Calvin Coolidge, John Milton, Walt Disney, Cotton Mather, Isaac Watts, Hubert Humphrey, Button Gwinnett, Samuel Adams, John Hancock, John Adams

"Pilgrims going to church"[99]

As is the case with Presbyterians, the United Church of Christ can trace its roots back to the Reformed Church of Zwingli and Calvin. The UCC as we know it today came into existence in 1957, when four denominations combined into one:

- Congregational Church

---

[99] Library of Congress LC-USZ62-3030

- Evangelical Church
- Christian Churches
- (German) Reformed Church in the U.S

The Congregationalists have as their ancestors the Puritans. As discussed in the section on the Baptists, the Puritans were a group within the Anglican Church that wanted to "purify" the church. More radical elements of the movement were called Separatists, who advocated a clean break from the Church of England.

In 1620, the Pilgrims, a radical offshoot of the Puritans, set sail for America on the *Mayflower*. Following close behind them in 1630 were another group of Puritans which established a colony in Massachusetts. These two groups would have great influence on religion and government in New England for the next 100 years.

Congregationalists believed in local autonomy for churches, adopted a Presbyterian form of government on a regional and national level, and were strict Calvinists. In fact, in the early years, Presbyterians and Congregationalists were closely associated in the Northeastern part of the United States.

Date	Event
1563	Puritans seek to "purify" the Anglican Church in England
1567	A group of Separatists calling themselves "The Privye Church" meet in London. Probably the first "Congregationalists".
1581	Robert Browne, an Anglican priest advocates Congregationalism in Norwich, England
September 6, 1620	Pilgrims embark for America aboard the Mayflower
November 11, 1620	*Mayflower Compact* signed, to "combine ourselves together into a civil body politic"
1630	Puritans embark for the New World
1634	Anne Hutchinson arrives in Massachusetts, and challenges the local Puritan hierarchy
October 1635	Roger Williams ejected from Massachusetts, after objecting to the lack of separation between church and state, and the seizing of land from the Indians. He would go on to create the colony of Rhode Island.
1636	Massachusetts Bay Colony votes to give £400 to establish a college in Cambridge, MA, named after early benefactor John Harvard
1637	Synod of the Bay Colony churches censors Anne Hutchin-

Date	Event
	son, who is eventually banned from the colony
1643	Members of the Presbyterian Westminster Assembly sign the Congregationalist *An Apologeticall Narration*
1646	"Corporation for the Promoting and Propagating of the Gospel of Jesus Christ in New England" formed to help spread the Gospel to the Indians
1649	English Puritans seize power after trying and executing Charles I
1660	End of Puritan rule in England
1662	Massachusetts adopts the "Half-Way Covenant", relaxing rules limiting church membership
1689	Puritan charter is revoked, guaranteeing other religious groups (Quakers, Baptists, Anglicans) religious freedom
1691 - 1692	Witchcraft trials in Salem; 19 executed for witchcraft
1705-06	Massachusetts adopts a plan formulated by Cotton Mather to require examination of ministers
1710	A Dutch Reformed minister, Paul Van Vlecq, assists a German congregation at Skippack, Pennsylvania
1734	Jonathan Edwards is a key figure in the *Great Awakening* in the United States
1740-1760	150 new Congregational churches formed[100]
September 24, 1747	Coetus (Council) of the Reformed Ministerium of the Congregations established in Pennsylvania for use by German Reformed Churches
c. 1793	The Synod of the German Reformed Church in United States of America formed; 178 German-speaking congregations and 15,000 communicant members existed[101]
1817	Evangelical Church of the Prussian Union created by order of Frederick William III (1797-1840) of Prussia, uniting the Lutheran and Reformed Churches
1825	German Reformed Church establishes a seminary in Carlisle, Pennsylvania
1826	The German Reformed Church Synod votes to create the American Missionary Society of the Reformed Church
1867	German Reformed Church drops the "German" from its name, and becomes the Reformed Church in the United States
June 25, 1957	Modern UCC church is founded
2006	The UCC has "6,500 congregations with approximately 1,800,000 members"[102]

---

[100] http://www.ucc.org/aboutus/shortcourse/cong.html
[101] http://www.ucc.org/aboutus/shortcourse/gerrefchu.html
[102] http://www.ucc.org/aboutus/shortcourse/early.html

Sources

- *A Brief History of Christian Baptism: From John the Baptist* to John Smyth by Robert C. Jones (Copyright 1998 by Robert C. Jones)
- *A New Evangelical Awakening*, Christian History & Biography Issue 92 (Fall 2006, Christianity Today)
- *A World Lit Only By Fire: The Medieval Mind and the Renaissance* by William Manchester (1992, Little Brown and Company)
- *American Puritans, The* Christian History 41 (1994, Christian History)
- *American Puritans, The*, Christian History Issue 41 (1994, Christian History)
- *American Religious Landscape and Political Attitudes: A Baseline for 2004, The* by John C. Green
- *American Revolution: Christianity's overlooked role in the bold venture to gain independence, The*, Christianity Today Issue 50 (1996, Christianity Today)
- *Bloody Theater or Martyrs Mirror, The* by Thielman J. van Braght (Herald Press)
- *Book of Discipline of The United Methodist Church – 2004, The* (United Methodist Publishing House, 2004)
- *Camp Meetings & Circuit Riders*, Christian History Issue 45 (1995, Christianity Today)
- *Charles Grandison Finney: 19th Century Giant of American Revivalism*, Christian History Issue 7 (1988, Christian History Institute)
- *Commentary on Romans* by Martin Luther (Kregel Publications, 1954/1976)
- *Creeds of Christendom: Vols. 1 & III, The* edited by Philip Schaff (Baker Books, 1931, 1996)
- *George Whitefield*, Christian History Issue 38 (1993, Christianity Today)
- *Handbook of Denominations in the United States*, by Frank S. Mead and Samuel S. Hill (Abingdon, 1995)
- Holy Bible - King James Version
- *Institutes of the Christian Religion*, by John Calvin, translated by Henry Beveridge (Wm. B. Eerdmans, 1995)
- *Jonathan Edwards: The Warm-Hearted Genius Behind the Great Awakening*, Christian History Issue 77 (2002, Christianity Today)
- *Martin Luther: The Later Years and Legacy*, Christian History Magazine (1993, Christian History)
- *Meet John Calvin*, Christian History Magazine (1986, Christian History Institute)
- *Membership*, 5/3/2003, United Methodist Church Archives
- *Monkey Trial & the Rise of Fundamentalism, The* , Christian History Issue3 55 (1997, Christianity Today)
- *Reformation, The* by Will Durant (MJF Books, 1957)
- *Rise of Pentecostalism, The* Christian History Magazine (1998, Christianity Today)
- *The Baptists: A People Who Gathered "To Walk in All His Ways.": Christian History, Issue 6*, (Carol Stream, IL: Christianity Today, Inc. 1997)
- *Theological Roots of the Protestant Reformation* by Robert C. Jones (Copyright 1996, 2005 by Robert C. Jones)

- *Untold Story of Christianity & the Civil War, The*, Christian History Issue 33 (1992, Christianity Today)
- *What Mennonites Believe* by J.C. Wenger (Herald Press, 1991)
- *William Tyndale: God's Outlaw*, Christian History Magazine (1987, Christian History Institute)
- *Zwingli: Father of the Swiss Reformation*, Christian History Magazine (1984, Christian History Institute)

Web sites:

- A Family Tree of Religious Groups (http://www.nazarene.org/archives/history/tree.pdf)
- A Short Course in the History of the United Church of Christ (http://www.ucc.org/aboutus/shortcourse/index.html)
- Assemblies of God – Our History (http://ag.org/top/about/history.cfm)
- Evangelical Lutheran Church in America Quick Facts (http://www.elca.org/communication/quick.html)
- Famous Adherents (http://www.adherents.com/adh_fam.html)
- Famous Lutherans (http://www.faithlutherangroton.org/famous.html)
- Famous Methodists (http://www.adherents.com/largecom/fam_meth.html)
- Famous Presbyterians (http://www.adherents.com/largecom/fam_pres.html)
- http://hirr.hartsem.edu/megachurch/definition.html
- http://www.law.umkc.edu/faculty/projects/ftrials/scopes/scopes2.htm
- http://www.pcusa.org/pcusa/info/women.htm
- http://www.robertperkinson.com/alcoholism_statistics.htm
- http://www.umc.org/churchlibrary/discipline/history/movement_toward_union.htm
- http://www.utm.edu/martinarea/fbc/bfm/6.html
- http://www.wikipedia.org/
- Largest Religious Groups in the United States of America http://www.adherents.com/rel_USA.html#2004total
- Methodist Church U.S.A. Archives (http://www.mcusa-archives.org)
- Presbyterian 101 (http://www.pcusa.org/101/101-whoare.htm)
- Religious Affiliation of U.S. Presidents (http://www.adherents.com/adh_presidents.html)
- The Lutheran Church--Missouri Synod At A Glance (http://www.lcms.org/pages/internal.asp?NavID=2436)
- United Methodist Church Archives (http://archives.umc.org/interior.asp?mid=1215)

About the Author

Robert C. Jones grew up in the Philadelphia, Pennsylvania area. In 1981, he moved to the Atlanta, Georgia area, where he received a B.S. in Computer Science at DeVry Institute of Technology. From 1984-2009, Robert worked for Hewlett-Packard as a computer consultant. He now works as an independent computer support and video services consultant.

Robert is an ordained elder in the Presbyterian Church. He has written and taught numerous adult Sunday School courses. He has also been active in choir ministries over the years, and has taught the Disciples Bible Study six times. He is the author of *A Brief History of Protestantism in the United States* and *Meet the Apostles: Biblical and Legendary Accounts*.

Robert is President of the Kennesaw Historical Society, for whom he has written several books, including *The Law Heard 'Round the World - An Examination of the Kennesaw Gun Law and Its Effects on the Community*, *Retracing the Route of the General - Following in the Footsteps of the Andrews Raid*, and *Images of America: Kennesaw*.

Robert has also written several books on ghost towns in the Southwest, including in Death Valley, Nevada, Arizona, New Mexico, and Mojave National Preserve.

In 2005, Robert co-authored a business-oriented book entitled *Working Virtually: The Challenges of Virtual Teams*.

His interests include the Civil War, Medieval Monasteries, American railroads, ghost towns, hiking in Death Valley and the Mojave, and Biblical Archaeology.

Robert is available as a guest speaker in the Atlanta/North Georgia area (robertcjones@mindspring.com).

Cover Photo: Acworth Presbyterian Church (founded 1870), Acworth, GA
(Photo by Robert Jones)

Made in the USA
Charleston, SC
22 January 2010